THE CARDINAL AND THE DEADLY

THE
CARDINAL
AND THE
DEADLY

Reimagining the Seven Virtues
and Seven Vices

Karl Clifton-Soderstrom

 CASCADE *Books* • Eugene, Oregon

THE CARDINAL AND THE DEADLY
Reimagining the Seven Virtues and Seven Vices

Cascade Books
An Imprint of Wipf and Stock Publishers
199 W. 8th Ave., Suite 3
Eugene, OR 97401

www.wipfandstock.com

ISBN 13: 978–1–61097–001–3

Cataloging-in-Publication data:

Clifton-Soderstrom, Karl

The cardinal and the deadly : reimagining the seven virtues and seven vices / Karl Clifton-Soderstrom.

x + 142 p. ; 23 cm. —Includes bibliographical references and index.

ISBN 13: 978–1–61097–001–3

1. Virtues. 2. Deadly sins. I. II. III. IV.

BV4626 .C65 2015

Manufactured in the U.S.A.   01/06/2015

For my parents,
with gratitude and love

Contents

ACKNOWLEDGMENTS

A FEW YEARS AGO, I was given an invitation to write a series of articles on the seven virtues and vices by Cathy Norman-Peterson, an editor for our denominational magazine, *The Covenant Companion*. This book is an outgrowth of that initial endeavor. I am grateful for Cathy's careful editing and insightful feedback during those 8 months of writing. Through the book project, her continued guidance through readings and conversations contributed much to my prose.

Several colleagues and friends have offered critique and ideas to my writing throughout this project. Kurt Peterson was an incisive reader of my work in its early stages, and key supporter throughout. My colleagues in the philosophy department, Greg Clark and Ilsup Ahn, also contributed to my writing through feedback sessions on specific chapters. Others including Mary Trujillo, Ron Dooley, Johnny Lin, Tim Lowly, Kristy Odelius, and Chad Eric Bergman were conversation partners in my thinking over the last couple of years.

Without the outstanding community of colleagues at North Park University and Theological Seminary, this project would not have begun or been completed. This community extends back to the initial introduction to virtue ethics given through my North Park professors Steven Bouma-Prediger and David Gill. Over the last several years, two key mentors contributed substantially to my philosophical investigation of the human person: Dr. Adriaan Peperzak at Loyola University Chicago and Mark Virshbo.

Special thanks must be given to Covenant Point Bible Camp in Iron River Michigan, where for three summers I would spend a week writing amidst the tall pines, cool waters, and exemplary staff. It offered the kind of Sabbath so needed for creative work.

I am thankful to those who teach me the most on the virtue of agape —my children Hannah and Johannes. They instruct me daily through their joy, creativity, and insights into the ways of grace. Finally, I must thank the most consistent and brilliant dialogue partner on all things theological and philosophical, my wife Michelle. From her own writings in theology and ethics, to our dinner conversations that mixed delight and debate, to the example of love and compassion she shows toward all she meets—Michelle is that ideal friend with whom I will be forever grateful to share a life.

1

ON BEING GOOD

VICTOR HUGO'S CLASSIC NOVEL and the now well-known theatrical piece *Les Misérables* recounts the fall and redemption of convicted thief Jean Valjean. Originally a good person of little financial means, Valjean is sentenced to five years for stealing a loaf of bread to feed his family. After several attempts to escape prison, however, he is kept behind bars for nineteen years.

Over those many years of incarceration, Valjean's moral disposition and character change from virtue to vice, from one inclined to seek goodness to one habituated to do evil. He becomes a hardened criminal whose tattered countenance is mean, suspicious, and deceitful. Upon being released from prison, he is friendless, without money or food, and carries within himself an acute awareness of his own desperate and contemptible state. "I am not even a dog," he laments to himself as person after person turns him away empty-handed.

At a crucial point in the story, Valjean is directed to a bishop in town who is known for his exceptional and long-standing humility, kindness, and good works for the poor and friendless in society. Without hesitation, and in full knowledge of Valjean's past life and recent incarceration, Bishop Myriel receives the convict and bestows dignity upon him by looking Valjean in the eye, sharing a meal using the finest silver, and inviting him to sleep the night in a bed with clean sheets. Overwhelmed, Valjean's countenance changes from gloom and resistance to gratitude and joy as he receives the bishop's

1

freely offered graces. His distant memory of experiencing these virtues in another human being is reawakened, and he receives and celebrates them with open arms and a full stomach.

Despite being returned to this long forgotten state of goodness, Valjean's nineteen-year habituation into a life of desperation, deception, and criminality while in prison remains potent. In the middle of the night, awakened by the sheer novelty of sleeping in an actual bed, Valjean can't help but think of the silver plates at the dinner table and the increasingly tempting possibility of stealing them to buy his own freedom. Daily bread is not enough for him, for he knows the long road ahead in his return to society. The newborn remembrance of his virtuous pre-prison life is no match for his now more hardened self-serving vices, and he steals the silver and flees the bishop's house.

As the story stands so far, it is tragic. The grace shown by the priest, many would say, was foolish. His virtue was no match for vice. There is, of course, more to the story, and we shall return to the crucial second encounter between the bishop and Valjean. But let us pause here to examine what this brief narrative tells us about how we experience and understand the moral life.

VIRTUE AND THE MORAL IMAGINATION

If you were to examine the potential this story holds for teaching us about the Christian life, what questions would you use to evaluate it? As I teach my students, *how* you ask your questions determines the range of possible answers. If you're not asking the right questions, you can't count on getting the right answers.

But how do you learn to ask the right questions that will disclose the right answers? This chicken-and-egg problem has been with philosophers and theologians from the beginning. While it seems like a silly paradox that modern people should dismiss, its analog in the moral life is quite significant. The father of philosophy, Plato, asked it in ancient Athens in a famous dialogue—*Meno*. How does knowledge begin? If I am ignorant of something, why would I seek to learn about it, for I could not know about that which I seek? But if I know what it is that I seek, why would I need to learn about it, since I already know what it is I want to know. Saint Augustine, in the first page of his *Confessions*, asks an analogous question with regard to the life of faith. Should we first seek help from God in order to know who God is, or must we first know who God is before we seek help? The parallel in the moral life might ask the question like this: If I do not yet know what a good life entails, why would I desire to live one? But if I know what a good life entails, I need not desire it, since I already know. Beginnings are always difficult—in knowledge, faith, or ethics.

Our biblical and theological heritage provides us with many tools for enabling ethical practices and ennobling moral character. Our heritage gives us the Ten Commandments, the Beatitudes in the gospels, stories of the heroes and saints of faith in *Acts*, sensible advice for individual churches and individuals in the epistles, the life of Jesus himself, and others. We could expand these options by considering how we learn from the history of the church in the various forms of Christian community, the councils and creeds, the history of individual saints, and the various rules, virtues, and admonitions given throughout the church's two-thousand-year history.

So let us begin more simply; by asking the right question. The two most basic questions that Christians face in the moral arena are "What should I do?" and "What kind of person ought I to become?" The first question focuses on specific actions and decisions; the second focuses on moral character and virtues.

If we are oriented by the fundamental task of doing the right thing, our reflections on the Christian life will focus on the particular actions and corresponding duties each of us should perform in a given context. Do not lie to your friend. Do not commit adultery against your spouse. Honor your father and mother. Give alms to the poor. In one framework of our contemporary moral imagination, a right action is determined by its coherence with a particular moral duty determined by some kind of moral law. This law might be given by God in the form of a command or mandate, as we have, for example, represented in the Ten Commandments. The law might also be given by the natural order of things, as for example, we have in the natural law tradition in ethics. Finally, the law might be given by Reason itself, as we have, for example, in the deontological tradition in ethics represented in the Universal Declaration of Human Rights. In the case of Jean Valjean. What should he do? Should he not steal *because* such an action is irreconcilable with this duty to obey the commandment of God, or the natural law protecting private property, or the law of reason that reveals the contradiction in affirming the need for private property and the freedom to steal it?

But you could also ask, Is stealing in accordance with the kind of person Jean Valjean would want to become? Thus one question we may ask is whether the scene from *Les Misérables* teaches us more about right actions or about good character?

Framing the moral life in terms of right and wrong actions that either do or do not correspond to a moral law is not the only way to understand ethics or a life faithful to God. If, for example, we desire to become *particular kinds of people*, say the people of God, disciples of Christ, or simply good persons, we seek to possess praiseworthy, admirable, and desirable character traits. As such, our descriptions of the Christian life will appeal to a vision of both human virtues and vices, of human excellences and depravities, of individual saints and scoundrels. Now of course, saints make good choices and perform right actions, but the goal of such actions is not the action itself, but the formation of good character or the flourishing of a good community. Broadly speaking, the virtue ethics tradition in Christian ethics frames the moral life in terms of the formation and sustaining of good character.

One particular tool for examining ourselves and our communities, which Christians have employed over the years, considers our *vices* and our *virtues*. "Tool" is not really the right word here, as if thinking about the moral life was merely a skill-set, a *techne*. There are as many virtues and vices as there are human excellences and depravities, and so, given the complexity of the human person, there is no set list (theologically speaking). Nevertheless, the Christian tradition often names seven virtues and seven vices. The virtues are divided up into four cardinal virtues (courage, temperance, justice, and wisdom) and three theological ones (faith, hope, and love). The vices are often called the "seven deadly sins."

But before we get ahead of ourselves, let us be a little more specific about virtues and vices. Broadly speaking, a virtue of a thing is what constitutes its distinctive excellence in view of its purpose or function. The virtue of a knife whose purpose is to cut is sharpness. Its vice is dullness. The virtues of a point guard in basketball whose purpose is to run the offense are agility and decisiveness. The virtue of a knife is not that of a point guard, which has different purposes and hence excellences.

The virtues of a human person are not as simple as those of a knife or a point guard. Our virtues are those distinct excellences of character through which we live into our moral and spiritual purposes well. According to broader Christian tradition, *a moral virtue is a settled disposition of a person to act in excellent and praiseworthy ways, cultivated over time through habit.* The constellation of virtues a person may embody provides for the organization of his or her moral desires, and hence, state of moral character.

For example, while a Christian may have a duty not to bear false witness in view of the commandment from God, God hopes for more than mere obedience to this commandment. Rather, God's desire is that every believer possesses the moral virtue of honesty. Honesty, when it is a virtue of one's character, is a basic, enduring, and identifying characteristic of the person. If you are honest, you don't lie one day, tell the truth the next day joyfully, and on the third day tell the truth begrudgingly. To be honest is to be so habituated to being honest that in any given situation, one consistently lives honestly without regret. Keep in mind, however, that in developing moral virtue, our emphasis is not on any particular action or decision, but on the cultivation of a moral identity from which the action comes "naturally." That last word, "naturally" is loaded philosophically, and we shall in the course of this book address the various meanings of acting "naturally."

Given this framework, we can understand the nature of human vices as well. A vice is a settled disposition of a person to act in inferior and abhorrent ways, cultivated over time through habit. If your vice is greed, you are inclined to be greedy rather than fair or generous. You may not constantly choose to hoard for yourself, but your character has been so shaped that selfish acquisition comes "naturally" to you. The seven vices, or deadly sins, are pride, greed, gluttony, sloth, anger, lust, and envy.

The Bible, of course, speaks of a wider variety of vices and virtues. Consider Colossians 3:5–14 as it describes the whole person, from the "old self" and its vices to the "new self" and its virtues:

> Put to death, therefore, whatever in you is earthly: fornication, impurity, passion, evil desire, and greed (which is idolatry). . . . But now you must get rid of all such things—anger, wrath, malice, slander, and abusive language from your mouth. Do not lie to one another, seeing that you have stripped off the old self with its practices and have clothed yourselves with the new self, which is being renewed in knowledge according to the image of its creator. . . . As God's chosen ones, holy and beloved, clothe yourselves with compassion, kindness, humility, meekness, and patience. Bear with one another and, if anyone has a complaint against another, forgive each other; just as the Lord has forgiven you, so you also must forgive. Above all, clothe yourselves with love, which binds everything together in perfect harmony.

In Victor Hugo's story, the bishop's enduring character, cultivated over time through habit, is one of humility, kindness, and compassion. The convict's moral identity is more complex because he has been formed by two narratives—his previous life as a virtuous and honorable man, and his nineteen years in prison as one habituated to deceit and selfishness that enabled him to survive a bad situation. The language of vice and virtue helps us to see that Jean Valjean's conflict that night at the bishop's house was less a choice between right and wrong actions—to steal or not to steal—than one between two moral identities. What kind of person would Jean Valjean become?

The real climax in this brief story occurs in their second encounter, where the bishop's virtues seize hold of Valjean's own soul, where a virtuous heart triumphs over a vicious one. After fleeing the bishop's house with the silver, Valjean is apprehended by the police and returned to the bishop with his fate all but sealed as a repeat offender returning to prison. But the bishop's virtue does not allow that to happen, for the bishop had seen the night before the memory of virtue sparked momentarily in Valjean, and he has compassion. In keeping with his virtue, the bishop *forgives* the convict.

Prominent Christian philosopher Jean Luc Marion writes that the essence of forgiveness is to give again that which was originally given but disregarded in ingratitude. But what is given again here from the virtuous priest to the vicious convict is Jean Valjean's own virtue, his own good soul, which was lost in memory over the course of those nineteen years but is now given back. Upon granting forgiveness, Bishop Myriel says to Jean Valjean, "Now, go in peace. . . . Forget not, never forget that you have promised me to use this silver to become a better man. . . . Jean Valjean, my brother, you belong no longer to evil, but to good. It is your soul that I am buying for you. I withdrew it from dark thoughts and from the spirit of perdition and I give it to God!"[1]

In the end, human virtues and vices teach us several things about the Christian moral life. First, these character traits mark an enduring individual moral identity. The bishop's virtues and the convict's vices, once acquired, are difficult to lose. Second, our virtues and vices are contagious and shape the character of those around us. The convict's character was shaped by his fellow prisoners, but it was also eventually converted by the bishop's virtue. Third, our moral virtues indicate to whom we belong, namely, to the good, to God. Throughout this book we shall consider each of these elements of vice and virtue with the hope of offering further discernment of how to live well as Christian people.

THE SCOPE AND DESIGN OF THE BOOK

Let us me establish a general working definition of virtue that can serve as a touchstone for the rest of the book. *Virtues are distinct human excellences of our moral, intellectual, and spiritual character that are praiseworthy, admirable, and desirable. They are cultivated over time through habit, sustained learning, and grace. Such virtues result in stable and effective dispositions to act and live toward goodness.*

1. Hugo, *Les Misérables*, 106.

In the course of this book, we will come to understand the various elements of this brief description in light of the Christian life. We will also see how this description has evolved over the course of the Christian tradition by indicating a few hallmark interpretations and debates. Finally, *and most importantly*, we will see the potential of this tradition to aid us to live more ethical and empathetic lives. The world is not divided up into priests and convicts, saints and sinners, virtuous and vicious people. We all, as individuals and communities, struggle to live out a more faithful, hopeful, and loving life in light of our fallenness and finitude. Too often, lists like the seven deadly sins have been used to shame and exclude some and laud and honor others. This books, in its phenomenology and content, hopes to prevent such simplistic bifurcations that do damage to our common life.

This book thus hopes to be both edifying and educative. It will be useful for students seeking a concrete introduction to virtue as a way of thinking ethically, and a good theological companion text to the primary texts it cites. The book should also be useful for individuals, pastors, and churches who are attempting to examine their own lives. It hopes to encourage readers in their efforts *to live* a more fulfilled and ethical life, and to help readers *to understand* an insightful mode of reflecting on that life. Aristotle and Aquinas, the two pillars in our tradition's systematic considerations of virtue, held that the well-lived life required formation in both moral and intellectual virtues. For human beings, with their distinctly rational nature, desire to understand all things, especially how to live well. And Aristotle and Aquinas saw that the otherwise good person could only be aided in their quest for a good life when they also cultivated an understanding of how and why to live such a life.

Contemporary Christian ethicist Jean Porter begins her overview of virtue ethics in a particularly clear and helpful way.

> Probably every society has identified certain human characteristics as being especially praiseworthy and worth cultivating, while also identifying others as vices, which are morally corrupt, contemptible or otherwise undesirable. These traditions of virtues, in turn, have frequently given rise to systematic reflection on what it means to be virtuous. . . . From the outset, Christians have identified certain traits of character as virtues which are distinctly characteristic of their way of life, while condemning others as vices which undermine the life of the soul and the well-being of the community. At some points, these Christian virtue traditions have given rise to systematic theories of virtue

in response to encounters with other traditions of virtue or to internal criticism and developments.[2]

In light of this overview, I might note three final aspects of the present project. First, while, as Porter notes, any given society has its own set of virtues and vices, this present book works within the broad Christian virtue tradition, with occasional reference to thinkers whose projects are not explicitly Christian nor on virtue (e.g., Aristotle, Frederich Nietzsche, Alasdair MacIntyre, Luce Irigaray, Immanuel Levinas). There is, of course, no single Christian tradition, but in view of a limited set of common Christian commitments and teachings—say the primary authority of Scripture, the person of Christ, and the major creeds of the church—we may speak, with appropriate intellectual humility, of something like "the church" or "the tradition" as the ongoing dialogue attempting to consciously live out of these commitments.

Any philosophical writing betrays its author's peculiar intellectual formation. My own formation stems from years in Protestant and Catholic universities and graduate schools. But most significantly, my moral imagination is informed by the denomination I have been a part of since my birth, the Evangelical Covenant Church. I hope the church's irenic commitment to seek theological truth through dialogue among a community of believers is present in this book as well. I might also say that though I myself am American and imagine a primarily American readership, I am not describing an American virtue ethic. Others, of course, have tried that whether it be Benjamin Franklin or William Bennett. My sources range from ancient Greek to contemporary French philosophers, from medieval theologians to American civil rights leaders, from poets to investment bankers. Among these sources, three thinkers will feature prominently in this book: Aristotle, the ancient Greek paragon of virtue ethics; St. Thomas Aquinas, the medieval synthesizer of Christian and Greek virtue ethics; and Martin Luther, the great reformer who challenged so much of Aristotelian thought. Together, these three thinkers expose the promise and limitations of a virtues approach to the moral life

Second, this project is organized around both an established set of identifiable virtues and vices (i.e., the big sevens) and a few noteworthy systematic reflections by philosophers or theologians. There are, of course, other virtues that contribute to a flourishing human life and faithful discipleship. These seven virtues and seven vices have, however, retained a cultural currency. For the last 1500+ years, these lists of seven have offered enduring wisdom into the moral anthropology of human beings as they

2. Porter, "Virtue Ethics," 96.

strive and falter in their desire for God. There continue to be a number of books published on the virtues and vices, though more often they are only on the vices or "seven deadly sins." We seem to like to read about those more often that the virtues. I do admit I find Dante's *Inferno* a much more interesting read than the *Paradisio*.

Third, in organizing the chapters around the fourteen character traits, I have broken them into six pairings with a single chapter on love. This is the unique philosophical angle this book on the virtues and vices takes that sets it apart from other approaches. Most books on the seven virtues or seven deadly sins either treat one set or the other, or, occasionally, treat them as a list of fourteen distinct character traits. The approach taken in this book pairs virtues and vices in new ways to reveal something more complex about the character of human desire. Each of these pairings will teach us something both particular to individual virtue/vice, as well as a way that some virtues may correct some vices. In this book, we seek a more nuanced analysis made available by discovering the "hinges" upon which pairs of virtues and vices swing. I take my lead from Luther who, in his commentary on Romans, states that pride and wisdom share a common hinge. The hinge is in how we understand our own humanity: pride distorts our view of humanity, wisdom sees it clearly. For sloth and faith, I will argue that the hinge is our receptivity to divine grace—sloth refuses to receive grace while faith embraces the divine gift. With regard to greed and hope, we discover in this odd pairing that hinge upon which they swing is *time*, or more precisely, the manner in which human beings live into time. In the end, each chapter reveals some key element of a virtues approach to ethics. The task of forming moral character is not simply swapping a virtue for a vice, but rather undertaking an iterative, imperfect, and holistic process that relies at every turn on divine grace.

In summary, the task of virtue ethics is to critically examine the character of human persons in terms of their dispositions and actions, by clarifying the distinct virtues that constitute a good life and vices that thwart it, so as to foster the intentional movement toward such a life. In the end, Christian virtue ethics is about forming disciples for Christ. In this book we shall participate in philosophical and theological conversation on the virtues and vices by utilizing the two lists of seven that have endured over the last two millennia. These two lists will be brought into explicit dialogue by pairing the virtues and vices. That said, I take seriously the theological critique of virtue language indicated by Martin Luther who said the movement of the people of God not only travels from vice to virtue but from virtue to grace. Throughout this text, we will wrestle with the relationship between grace and virtue.

Our task here is to think and imagine. What follows are neither doctrines nor moral rules. As Luther notes in his commentaries on Genesis, human beings are *animal rationale, habens cor fingens.* We are beings furnished with reason who have a heart that imagines, makes pictures, and invents. The tradition of seven virtues and seven vices is the result of such imaginings of the human heart in its desire to understand itself. My task in this book is to engage my readers' reason and moral imagination so that we may respond in gratitude and creativity to the ethical challenges of living together.

2

ON BEING HUMAN
Pride and Wisdom

To say more than human things with human voice,
That cannot be; to say human things with more
Than human voice, that, also, cannot be;
To speak humanly from the height or from the depth
Of human things, that is acutest speech.

—WALLACE STEVENS, "CHOCORUA TO ITS NEIGHBOR"

I S PRIDE A VICE or a virtue?
A father watches anxiously as his twenty-six-year-old son positions himself at the starting blocks of the 400-meter race. It is the 1992 Olympic Games in Barcelona. Jim Redmond has supported his son Derek's running career from the beginning. In this moment Jim swells with pride at his son's achievements. Derek has made the Olympics, he has broken the British records for the 400-meter, and won gold medals in the European and International championships. In this moment, Jim's son Derek possesses the beauty and severity of a young man in his athletic prime.

The starting gun fires. Derek Redmond takes off down the track, determined to continue his phenomenal success. Midway through the race, however, Derek tears a muscle in his leg and collapses. The upward trajectory of his success halts suddenly, and his body and spirit lay prostrate on the track as his competitors race to the finish. With no hope of earning anything other than last place, Derek pulls himself up and hobbles down the track toward the finish line. He falters again in weeping agony and stops. Meanwhile, Derek's father Jim sprints down from the upper rows of the stands and leaps over the barrier surrounding the track to join his son. With 100 meters left between Derek and the finish line, Jim reaches Derek, puts his arm around his defeated son, and the two of them finish the race together in sweat, pain, and tears.

What were Jim and Derek experiencing in these moments? Was Jim's pride in his son dashed? If Derek earned his father's pride through his own achievements, did Jim have to swallow his pride in order to assist his son? Later, Jim would tell the press, "I'm the proudest father alive. I'm prouder of him than I would have been if he had won the gold medal." What about Derek? His upward climb in the racing world stopped as quickly as his own physical momentum that day. Did he lose all sense of pride in this moment? Or, was it pride that enabled Derek to finish the race? If his pride strengthened his resolve to get back up and finish, did he have to give up his pride when he allowed his father to help him?

The ancient Greeks knew well that the Olympics could showcase the glory, nobility, and magnificence of humanity. In their political community, defined by agonistic rituals of skill and honor, the Olympics offered an arena to witness the best in strength, stamina, and speed. In the year 2000, the International Olympic committee continued this humanistic perspective in their marketing of the Olympics. Their ad campaign, named "Celebrate Humanity," featured Derek Redmond's race in its opening montage, though it did not show his father's assistance. It highlighted, rather, Derek picking himself after his first collapse. Humanity, the advertisement and others in the series told us, is magnificent to behold. But how magnificent was Derek Redman's humanity in that moment? Was not the winner of the race a better representative of the glorious human spirit? Certainly if the ancient Olympians had had an ad campaign, those Greeks would have shown the victor, who in their minds deserved his pride.

THE COMPLEXITY OF PRIDE

When we consider the list of seven vices, pride seems the most unlikely to be a sin at all. Envy, gluttony, lust, and greed are perhaps obviously all vices. But pride? What about the pride a parent has for a child? The pride citizens take in their nation? Black pride? Is it wrong to be proud to be a Christian? Certainly arrogance is ugly; vanity is laughable; conceitedness is unsociable. But pride? Compared to these synonyms, it appears outright noble. In his short book titled *Pride*, Georgetown sociologist Michael Eric Dyson considers contemporary racial pride alongside more ancient Christian and Greek traditions. "If pride is a sin," Dyson writes, "it is no ordinary sin, to be sure."[1] But why the confusion?

Understood in a psychological sense, pride is neither virtue nor vice, but simply a healthy and necessary attitude about one's own worth, accomplishment, or merit. Feeling pride in one's child for their gifts, or in one's neighborhood for its sense of tradition, or in oneself for achieving some hard-earned goal, are all fitting emotional responses. In an elegant phrasing, psychologist Gabrielle Taylor notes that such "pride expresses a due sense of our own force and so amounts to proper self-esteem."[2] For those prone to self-loathing, doesn't the feeling of pride mark a movement toward health? Within our democratic culture, isn't pride exactly what abused or disenfranchised groups need in this world? Doesn't it provide strength amidst trial?

In a sociological framework, pride is often used as something akin to dignity. In the example of "Black Pride," Dyson expands from the individual sense of self-esteem to a social one. "Black pride, whether it concerns our skin, our politics, our social order, our culture, or our stories of overcoming, is rooted in our will to be as free as possible to love ourselves without apology or regret."[3] The moral and political struggles carved out by heroes and saints are a necessary part of Black self-respect and self-esteem. Contemporary theologian Rosemary Radford Reuther has spoken of the dignity inherent in pride and hence critiqued some of the Christian rhetoric around pride. She has argued that the pride–humility paradigm needs to be re-imagined for women, and by extension, for other marginalized persons who traditionally are only deemed virtuous by having no self of their own. As agents in our own lives, as inheritors of a past, as parents and educators of an emerging generation, proper pride duly acknowledges our agency as human beings.

1. Dyson, *Pride*, 5.
2. Taylor, *Deadly Sins*, 71.
3. Dyson, *Pride*, 84

In the philosophical tradition, pride also enjoys a certain privileged place. For Aristotle and the Greeks, pride was noble. Aristotle claimed, "The proud man, then, is an extreme in respect of the greatness of his claims, but a mean [i.e., fitting] in respect of the rightness of them; for he claims what is in accordance with his merits."[4] David Hume assumed pride a virtue, and a far preferable character trait to humility, its opposite. Nietzsche, that nineteenth-century German so inspired by heroic Greek culture, claimed that Christianity made vices out of humanity's greatest virtues, and thought this was nowhere more so than with pride. Through Nietzsche's character Zarathustra, Nietzsche writes, "A new pride my ego taught me, and this I teach men: no longer to bury one's head in the sand of heavenly things, but to bear it freely, an earthly head, which creates a meaning for the earth."[5]

Though the meaning of pride in our cultural imaginations is often positive, in the context of Christian literature, pride is a cardinal vice, perhaps even *the deadliest* of the seven. Due in no small part to St. Augustine and the larger Medieval context that solidified the place of the seven virtues and vices in our imagination, the Christian church has given pride, well, pride of place in the list of vices. As a vice, it rules above all others. The question remains, is the Christian tradition simply what Nietzsche makes it out to be—a moral system whose only genius is that it managed to take our best virtues and turn them into vices? If the Christian tradition does not merely seek to deny the dignity of the human person, then pride *as a vice* must indicate something different than our psychologists, sociologists, and philosophers have seen. What is it that the Christian tradition has seen in this vice, and how may it be uncovered without resorting to caricatures? We should not carelessly dismiss or praise pride. Our task here is to see more of the vice's complexity. Oversimplifying human vices and virtues only results in harmful demonization or idealization of others, and that certainly is no virtue.

When considering pride's complexity as a vice, it is helpful to bring it into dialogue with the virtue of *wisdom*. Wisdom is the hallmark virtue of human beings as creatures endowed with the rational capacity of forethought and planning, memory and learning, and the abilities to manipulate and organize the natural and cultural world. We are *Homo sapiens*, wise humans, a distinct development from both *Homo erectus*, upright humans, and *Homo habilis*, tool using humans. The fruitfulness of examining pride and wisdom together is that pride and wisdom *are a distinctly human vice and virtue*. I take my cue from the reformer Martin Luther, who notes in the

4. Aristotle, *Nicomachean Ethics*, 1104a.
5. Solomon and Higgins, *What Nietzsche* Really *Said*, 193.

opening to his commentary on *Romans* that wisdom and pride share a common *hinge*. That hinge swings on the question of how we are to understand and respect our humanity.

There is another promise for pairing these two character traits that is rather ironic. Whether we look to Christian *superbia* or Greek *hubris*, pride is the distinctly human delusion that *we can transcend our humanity*. Thinkers as diverse as Aristotle, Luther, and Nietzsche note the very human desire to become godlike. Aristotle found the desire to understand and gain wisdom itself something divine in the human, but still fraught with risk and antisocial tendencies. Martin Luther considered the human temptation to not "let God be God" outright sinful and precisely what led Adam to fall. Nietzsche saw the human capacity to be more than human our chief source of greatness.

In the context of this book, we begin with wisdom and pride because of the project of virtue ethics itself. The virtues of a good life must be grounded in a characteristically *human life*, and a consideration of *wisdom* enables us to focus on a distinctly human excellence. If our traditions are correct, pride too is characteristically human. Examining the pair of wisdom and pride will illuminate the first of two grounds to imagining our moral character: human nature.

Aristotle on Magnanimity and Hubris

In Ancient Greece, pride was more than a healthy sense of self; it was a virtue. To appreciate the Greek conception of pride as a distinctive excellence worthy of imitation, we must remember its aristocratic culture. Werner Jaeger notes, "The history of Greek culture actually begins in the aristocratic world of early Greece, with the creation of a definite ideal of human perfection."[6] This aristocratic ideal found its most natural expression in the idea of *arête*, which in its oldest meaning entailed a proud and courtly morality combined with warlike valor. Aristotle, a late inheritor of this tradition, retrieved this warrior imagery and reinterpreted it for his own peaceful, civic, and aristocratic setting. For the aristocrats of Aristotle's Athens, pride was the magnanimous (*megalopsychia*) character of the great-souled man. In such a person, high-mindedness marked a confident self-respect befitting one's well established moral and intellectual excellence.

In such a context, proper pride rises above vanity's foolishness, and attains an honest sense of confidence about one's own achievement. For Aristotle, the magnanimous person is truly virtuous, having cultivated his

6. Jaeger, *Paideia*, 4.

capacities for all things deemed noble and good in accordance with his humanity and within his moral community. Imagine someone you admire, someone who embodies many qualities of solid character, good spirit, and sharp intellect. Why, Aristotle would ask, would we consider humility or self-abasement admirable for *this* kind of person? That said, Aristotle notes that proper pride is no easy task. In keeping with his desire to celebrate human greatness and the positive role heroes play in the moral imagination of a culture, Aristotle requires that the proud be *morally good and just* to the highest degree. Vanity and false humility benefit neither the individual nor their community. A good community requires honest self-perception among the ordinary among us, and appropriate pride among the heroic and gifted. It is thus difficult to be truly proud, because it is difficult to be truly good.

Understood as magnanimity, we can see why Aristotle would consider pride a virtue. For all his endorsement of magnanimity as the virtue befitting the noble, Aristotle certainly warned against *hubris*. Most commonly cited as the chief fault of the tragic hero in Greek narratives, *hubris* is excessive arrogance and overreaching ambition. Such conceit in the otherwise gifted hero results in insolence toward cultural codes, ethical boundaries, and in the end, the gods themselves. Hubris is the vicious disposition toward one's own self that leads in the opposite direction of magnanimity. Where the magnanimous achieve rightful recognition for exemplary character befitting the culture of Greek aristocracy, those with hubris see themselves *outside* the moral community. Such vice tempts its bearer to shame others within the community in order to give the perception that they are beyond it. It destroys individual souls and, when such individuals hold power in society, whole communities.

Augustine on Pride

In contrast to the classical Greek view of the magnanimous aristocrat, a longstanding Christian tradition cannot see such a person as the exemplar for the human person. Though Christ was the "King of kings," he was no aristocrat. Rather, as Paul writes in Philippians 2:7, he humbled himself and "did not count equality with God as something to be grasped, but emptied himself, taking the form of a servant." He rode into Jerusalem on a donkey at the start of his most celebrated week, and was crucified at the end of it. With such passages informing the Christian moral imagination, "pride" is named as the root of all other sins and the vice *par excellence*. To understand this bold claim better, we look back to St. Augustine from whom much of our contemporary understanding of pride stems.

Augustine is well known for his preaching on the virtues and against the vices, most notably against pride and lust. As a brilliant and accomplished preacher, scholar, and rhetorician, living in the greatest (albeit waning) empire in the world, Augustine knew well the temptations and trappings of pride. The Roman Empire inherited much from the Greeks, including a culture based on honor and a strong sense of its own self-importance. Augustine's personal difficulty with pride makes sense given his own high social, educational, and ecclesial status, but also having grown up amidst the empire's own lust for domination and its celebrated heroes' desire for praise and public honors. Augustine saw these tendencies clearly in his culture and himself, and brought a Christian corrective to bear.

For Augustine, vicious pride disposes one to continuously replace the love of God with love of self. As such, the prideful self perpetually forgets the absolute distance between God and humanity. It denies our creaturliness and attempts to elevate our humanity to the status of the Creator by assigning to humanity functions only God can properly fulfill.

While we often perceive pride through another's arrogant emotions or belligerent actions, Augustine locates pride in our distorted understanding of reality. Pride fails to live according to the hierarchy of being. The hierarchy of being is a term often used to describe Augustine's classical view of the structure of reality. In the logic of the hierarchy, God is the highest good, whereas inert matter is, roughly speaking, the lowest good. Human beings, animals, angels, etc. exist in between, since they are neither the Creator nor base matter. When living fully into one's humanity, a person recognizes the distinction between creature and Creator, and loves each according to its being. God as the highest good, the source of all goodness, is to be loved in an unqualified sense above all else. In the prideful self, however, the love of self competes with and even subsumes the love of God. This is not simply a disordered affection, but a distorted understanding of reality, a kind of spiritual and philosophical schizophrenia. The prideful act as if they are the source of goodness, the source of their own power, and the Creator of their own moral values. Humanity, as the *imago Dei*, should take its grounding reference and purpose from God itself. We are only an image of God, and a cracked image at that. In the end, pride distorts our image of ourselves by alienating us from what would make us most happy. Ironically, it results in an impossible self love, since that which makes us lovable—the *imago Dei* itself—is denied.

The Christian tradition has inherited Augustine's argument against pride, and it would do us well to remember this. Of course, we become most aware of vicious pride when we encounter it in others as a kind of public boasting, chest thumping, or other palpable display of bragging. But as with many of the seven vices, pride enters our own lives with more subtlety. Pope Gregory claimed pride occurs when a person "favors himself in his thought: and walks with himself along the broad spaces of his thought and silently utters his own praises."[7] The turn toward the self becomes particularly tempting not only in our individualistic American culture, but among my own evangelical and Pietist traditions. Those of us who emphasize a personal God, a personal story of salvation, and a personal relationship to our Redeemer cannot help but be faced with the temptations of pride that accompany such an elevation of self in the Christian life. Augustine himself solidified the genre of the spiritual autobiography that has come to shape much of our Christian view of the self. Augustine would recognize the risks of our own post-Reformation faith. The problem, of course, is not in making my religious faith personal to me and to my story. The problem is the temptation to make the Christian life ultimately about me and not about the Creator.

As an individual vice, pride is the soul's turning away from God and toward the self. Pride entails a conversion that mimics and distorts one's conversion to Christ. Pride de-centers our soul's orientation such that the prideful person perceives and acts as if he or she is at that center of existence. Placing oneself at the center, the prideful are unable to see reality as it really is, because as contemporary Christian ethicist William Mattison says, pride sees "all of reality through the warped lens of 'what does it have to do with me.'"[8] For the individual Christian, *pride becomes a fixation on one's own life and desires.* This fixation engenders outright aversion to the commands of God and the place the self has in the divine order. In the end, pride blinds one to the wisdom into the source of all goodness in God, deafens one to God's commands, and desensitizes one to the needs of one's neighbor. Pride misperceives reality for what it is and thus obscures the clarity all virtues need to flourish.

WISDOM AND PRUDENCE

In this book, our task is not simply to illuminate the character of the vices, but to get a sense of the complexity of the moral life by juxtaposing the vices and virtues. With some grasp on the Augustinian interpretation of pride as the failure to live within our own creatureliness, we turn now to wisdom.

7. Gregory, *Moralia in Job*, cited in Lyman, *Seven Deadly Sins*, 136.
8. Mattison, *Introducing Moral Theology*, 237.

In the list of seven, while pride is the root of all human vice, wisdom is the preeminent *human* virtue and a fitting antidote to pride. This claim may seem misplaced. For it appears that pride is a problem of attitude not aptitude. Each of us probably knows a smart but arrogant person or two— the last thing they need is more intelligence! Rather, we might argue, what they really need is humility. But humility as the sheer negation of pride can just as easily steer us wrongly. Humility can degrade into a humiliating self-abasement, which, Aristotle was right to note, demands no respect. Humility for humility's sake does not encourage either the further cultivation of virtue nor the receptivity to grace. The key to cultivating the virtues is to appreciate them as interconnected within the moral imagination. Blocking the vices outright leaves the person with no means of imagining their way toward the good. So, while humility is indeed a corrective to pride, we must be more nuanced about what we mean by humility. This is where wisdom becomes relevant. I claim, along with Augustine and Bernard of Clairvaux, that wisdom is precisely the form of humility most suited to countering pride. For if pride is the initial distortion of our own humanity, wisdom is the initial corrective.

You may consider pausing here to consider two questions: Who do you consider wise? How is their wisdom manifest? In considering the wise, and not simply the intelligent or the genius, we note that wisdom informs us on how to live in the immediate context of the here-and-now. The "wisdom" of the seven virtues is *prudence*. *Prudence* is the English translation of the Latin *prudentia* used by Roman and Medieval Christian thinkers. *Prudentia* was itself rooted in the term *phronesis* used by the Ancient Greeks. According to our current sensitivities, "prudence" gets coupled with "prude" and "priggish," which connote excessive attention to propriety. The etymology of "prudence," however, suggests a richer meaning than the present-day connotations indicate. In its classical meaning, a prudent person possess a brilliance more akin to jazz improvisation than a stodgy adherence to traditional codes of conduct. As such, prudence does not look backward but forward. Prudence is analogous to how a musician can be so attuned to the present performance of their bandmates, that they can move into the future of the piece by improvising something both creative and fitting.

Prudence, as practical wisdom, is the intellectual virtue connected to moral action. Though celebrated as the highest of the cardinal virtues, it remains grounded in the earthly everyday. It thus bridges knowledge of the holistic purpose of human life with the commonplace experience of the present. It directs our attention, emotion, and action to what the situation we are experiencing in this moment demands. Prudence thus guides the enactment of all other virtues. Virtue—any virtue whether it be courage, temperance, or justice—must be attained in *this* life, among *these* people, in *these* times, and in *these* situations. Without being able to navigate all the messy particularities of one's life and culture, no person would attain virtue, let alone live very long. And so to begin our consideration, we may note that wisdom's gift to us is a kind of double vision: insight into the whole of life and attention to its particulars.

Aristotle on Prudence

For Aristotle, prudence (*phronesis*) is an excellence particular to a rational soul. Along with other Athenian philosophers, Aristotle understood rationality as the distinctive and essential characteristic of humanity. The rational soul thinks, plans, chooses, knows, argues, and understands the order of nature and how to manipulate it. Such a soul, however, doesn't just think, but acts. Thus, the merit of *phronesis* is how it connects thinking about humanity and the world with acting humanly in the world. In most meaningful situations in life, however, where doing the right thing *really matters*, determining the right course of action is difficult. As Aristotle says,

> Fear, confidence, appetite, anger, pity and in general pleasure and pain can be experienced too much or too little, and in both ways, not well. But to have them at the right time, about the right things, toward the right people, for the right end, and in the right way is the mean and best; and this is the business of virtue.[9]

The difficulty, according to Aristotle, is that because every action takes place in a *particular* situation, there is no rule book for handling the complex settings that demand moral choice and action. Success depends on a host of judgment calls that are attentive and responsive to the unique situation at hand. Wisdom consists in consistently making good judgments.

Lest this insight seem too general to be helpful, imagine someone you believe to be wise. What does such a person do when they display wisdom? According to Aristotle, the practically wise person possess three traits. First, they possess a holistic understanding of the good of a human life. The practically wise person knows something more than *how* to act in a given situation; she knows *why* one should act. In order to know *why* one should act, one needs to know the end toward which one's actions are directed. For Aristotle, all virtuous actions aim toward a single end: human flourishing, or happiness (*eudaimonia*). When facing a moral dilemma of how to act, the

9. Aristotle, *Nicomachean Ethics*, II.6.

wise already possess some knowledge of a good and flourishing human life. They possess a foresight into the *telos* of human desire before they interpret the particular situation at hand. Happiness is not just a content or positive feeling about one's situation in life, it is the activity of living well into our distinctly human nature and its moral purposes. The possessor of practical wisdom consistently chooses the right course of action in a particular situation in light of the holistic good of human flourishing. André Comte-Sponvill elegantly summarizes it when he notes that *phronesis* "could be called good sense, but in the service of good will."[10]

Second, the wise person also *deliberates* about the course of action in light of this overall good. The wise don't just happen to make good decisions, they do so consciously. People make right decisions all the time, but some are made out of blind obedience to some rule, others from sheer dumb luck, and others for the wrong reasons. Celebrating right action alone reduces morality to adherence to rules, and risks sacrificing the well being of real people to moral absolutes. The wise deliberate over the multiple goods at hand, utilizing their intellect and desire for the good, and choose a course of action.

Third, the wise *choose* to act and not merely speculate. The prudent are often patient enough to observe carefully and see multiple possible actions, but in the end, they choose. Their moral decisions in concrete lived experiences are precisely *choices* because they must be made in the absence of proof or certainty. Prudence recognizes that contingency, risk, uncertainty, and chance describe most of our important life choices, and thus it assesses the real risks of a given decision, which cannot be completely avoided, and chooses the best course of action. With the overarching good of human flourishing in mind, the wise are attentive not myopic, responsive not reactive, creative not rigid.

Both Greek and Christian traditions give wisdom a priority of place among the four cardinal virtues: wisdom, courage, temperance, and justice. Appreciating this priority is helpful in understanding why wisdom is well suited to counter the vice of pride. First, Aristotle recognizes prudence as an *executive virtue* for all other virtues. Christian theologian Thomas Aquinas will say something similar one thousand years later. Without prudence, the just person would not know how to act for the cause of justice, the courageous would not know when to risk harm to defend the good, the generous would not know for whom to provide, and the loving would not know to love this person in a way befitting of overall happiness. Second, prudence does not exist itself apart from any other virtue. There is no generic practical

---

10. Comte-Sponville, *Small Treatise on the Great Virtues*, 32.

wisdom that helps us discern what it means to live well into some abstract "life as such." Rather, practical wisdom is achieved alongside the realization of any particular virtue that directs our desires toward some more particular end. Prudence both governs and serves the other virtues. Third and finally, according to Aristotle, practical wisdom is what makes all the virtues *human*. For the Greek tradition that we inherited, this is because prudence requires choice, rational deliberation, and insight into the final ends of humanity. For example, courage becomes *human* courage when it is habituated over time and allows our inherent rationality to be acted upon in excellent ways. A truly courageous act requires a situation that must be deliberated over using the powers of reason, weighed in light of the overall good of human flourishing, and is then chosen as the excellent and praiseworthy action. None of this would be possible without the intrinsic inclusion of the intellect with our practices. In the end, practical wisdom enables all the virtues to flower into their full brilliance in such a way that our humanity shines forth.

Consider the following example. Imagine that you have been wronged in some way—you have been cheated out of some deserved compensation at school or work, you have been publicly slandered, or you have been bullied by a fellow student or colleague. In response to that harm, you become angry. In keeping with his doctrine of the mean, Aristotle argued that vicious anger arises when we feel it too little by responding with apathy toward the wrong, or too much by responding with rage disproportionate to the offence. Virtuous anger, what some in the Christian tradition call righteous anger, entails experiencing anger about the right things, toward the right people, for the right end, and in the right way, and sustains that anger for the right amount of time.[11] In order to be virtuous in this situation with regard to anger, we require the *judgment of practical wisdom* to move from that feeling to a chosen action. Our chosen response becomes virtuous because we make a judgment call that results from our deliberation on the situation and valuation of some good, e.g., the preservation of human community. How does one make that judgment? The solution is not that one should be mildly angry about most things, neither too angry (enraged) nor not angry enough (sheepish). But one should be appropriately angry *in the particular situation given to us*. Certainly some situations necessitate a great deal of anger, while others demand merely mild disappointment. The judgment of how to be angry, and how to act in light of that anger, requires the ability to *understand* the context and the appropriate way in which one's desires can

11. Aristotle, *Nicomachean Ethics*, 1106a.

be truthful to the situation and the soul. This is the executive function that wisdom offers to the rest of the virtues.

Aquinas and Bernard: Wisdom's Humility

The intentional structure of prudence that I have laid out does not yet indicate fully why it serves as an antidote to pride. Here we turn to Christian interpretations of wisdom that build upon Aristotle, but offer something more. While there is some shared insight between the Greek and Christian traditions into prudence, there are key differences that demonstrate why wisdom both reveals the nature of pride and counters it. In an effort to highlight these differences, we look to Thomas Aquinas and Bernard of Clairvaux.

One key insight that Aquinas offers to the Aristotelian description of prudence is that the wise are *docile*. For us, docility evokes connotations of passivity, submissiveness, and quietism. Even more pejorative, we might imagine the docile to be sheepish or cowardly. In the service of Aquinas' argument, however, docility has a more positive significance. To be docile is to be *teachable* and ready for instruction. "Docile" (teachable) and "docent" (teaching guide) stem from the same Latin root, *docere* "to teach." Docents require docile students, and vice versa. With regard to wisdom, the wise act not only upon what they have learned, but humble themselves perpetually in order to remain teachable. The docility of wisdom marks not only a necessary attitude *on the way to* wisdom, but a defining characteristic of the virtue itself. As such, wisdom is a virtue that is never finished being cultivated. The reasons for this are not only that the human mind intrinsically desires further understanding, but also because the particularities of life that demand wise decision-making are never static. The world is complex in its details, and those details are ever in flux. As Aquinas argues, "Prudence is concerned with particular matters of action, and since such matters are of infinite variety, no one man can consider them all sufficiently; nor can this be done quickly, for it requires length of time. Hence in matters of prudence, man stands in very great need of being taught by others, especially by old folk who have acquired a sane understanding of the ends in practical matters."[12] So the wise must be docile in their receptivity and attentiveness to the phenomena of experience, in order that they may be present to the situation at hand. To become and remain prudent, one must also remain teachable by others. The prudent learn wisdom communally, that is through the passage of wisdom from one generation to the next. The

---

12. Aquinas, *Summa Theologia*, II-II.49.3.

proud are precisely those who mistake their limited wisdom for certainty and absolute truth; they refuse to see the truth that others see.

A second insight of Aquinas concerns the relation between wisdom and the ends of human life. The wise, as we noted, are blessed with a double vision: they see the whole and the particular. In this regard, Aquinas notes that wisdom is preeminent among the four cardinal virtues. Like Aristotle, Aquinas holds that our virtues are nested within one another and depend ultimately on prudence to order them well—for prudence not only *sees* the right course of action but also how that particular good contributes to the overall human good.[13] While Aristotle too recognized this about wisdom, Aquinas offers a different view of what makes us human. As much as rationality is praised in both biblical and theological traditions as one of the greatest divine gifts to humanity, rationality does not sufficiently represent the *imago Dei*. Rather, *love of God and neighbor* is a higher, more encompassing end than rationality because *love* marks the most encompassing character of God. Aquinas quotes Augustine in subordinating knowledge to love: "prudence is love choosing wisely."[14] The love of God orients *all* ends and pursuits, and the love of neighbor perfectly expresses that love in the particularity of our earthly life. Prudence, you could say, understands how love can become manifest through our wise actions in the world. It is the wisdom of love, to re-order the traditional translation of *philosophia* as love-of-wisdom. Here we see how wisdom is the corrective of pride. If pride places the self at center stage, the wisdom of love places love-of-God and love-of-neighbor at the center. This will be explained more fully in the final chapter of this book.

The final corrective the Christian tradition offers vis-à-vis Aristotle and the Greek view of wisdom concerns the *humility of wisdom*. In this attribute, we find a final insight that prudence offers to the proud: the wise know themselves. For this insight, we look to Bernard of Clairvaux who explicitly connected the virtues of wisdom and humility.[15] In his sermon on the Song of Songs, Bernard considers humility a distinct form of wisdom:

> There are then different kinds of knowledge, one contributing to self-importance, the other to sadness. Which of the two do you think is more useful or necessary to salvation, the one that makes you vain or the one that makes you weep? . . . [Paul] does

13. Aquinas, *Summa Theologia*, I-II.57.5

14. Aquinas, *Summa Theologia*, I-II.47.

15. Bernard is not alone in this idea. In the Christian tradition, others have considered humility both an affect of the heart and a form of wisdom. Solomon himself notes in Prov 11:2, "When pride comes, then comes disgrace; but wisdom is with the humble."

not forbid thinking, but inordinate thinking. And what is meant
by thinking with sober judgment? It means taking the utmost
care to discover what are the essential and primary truths, for
time is short. . . . There is nothing more effective, more adapted
to the acquiring of humility, than to find out the truth about
oneself. . . . If you lack self-knowledge you will possess neither
the fear of God nor humility.[16]

As we noted above, Augustine taught that when prideful, a person
becomes so consumed with their own self that their mind becomes subject
to inferior things, like one's own creaturliness, rather than to the superior
thing of the Creator. The wisdom of humility knows one's place in creation
and is thus free to be formed by that which is superior to self, namely God.
Bernard's command to "know thyself" was very much tied to his other ad-
monition to "be humble." He and Martin Luther both held that *humility is
self-knowledge perfected*. Of course, Socrates too connected wisdom with
the command he received from the Oracle at Delphi to "know thyself." But
for Bernard, and those in the Christian tradition, to know oneself means to
know oneself in relation to God. Self-knowledge does not entail one's identity as an individual personality or Myers-Briggs type, for the self's deep-
est identity is one dependent upon the Creator and redeemer of humanity.
Therefore, to know oneself in relation to God renounces the human person's
self-sufficient merits before God and demands reliance upon divine grace.
Bernard writes on this connection between humility and self-knowledge,

> There is nothing more effective, more adapted to the acquiring
> of humility, than to find out the truth about oneself. There must
> be no dissimulation, no attempt at self-deception, but a facing
> up to one's real self without flinching and turning aside.[17]

According to Bernard, prudent action requires humility. To be humble
is to know oneself as a creature of God, and servant to others, and in the
end, perpetually dependent upon divine grace in all these endeavors. St.
Paul is fond of berating a kind of knowledge that merely "puffs up." Yet we
seek a wisdom that grounds us in the reality of our creaturliness. Augustine
notes when someone turns toward themselves in pride (as opposed to humility), that person does not see the whole self since what it means to be a
self is bound to our source, our Creator. Prideful persons have a distorted
view of self, not only when they puff up their own virtues inaccurately, but

---

16. Bernard, *Commentary on the Song of Songs*, Sermon 36.2.
17. Ibid., 36.5.

when they are ignorant of their dependence upon the God as the source of all good gifts.

CONCLUSION

To conclude, as we consider this first pairing of pride and wisdom, perhaps the simplest way to put it is that *pride is arrogant ignorance*. Pride entails an inability to see things as they truly are, particularly oneself as a creature of God, and pride is thus blind to the good. Wisdom is the virtue of those who know and recognize the truth, which in turn enables the performance of all the other virtues. Wisdom, as correct vision of the good and our place in the divine order, turns our hearts and minds back to God, the source of all excellence and virtue.

These insights allow us to see the distinction between pride as a vice, and how we use the term "pride" in more virtuous ways. For example, the "pride" that a disenfranchised group truly needs is really a form of courageous wisdom that seeks justice for their rightful place in the world. The "pride" that virtuous people have for their own goodness or the goodness of their community is really a wisdom that knows that all goodness originates in God. The "pride in self" that the lost and depressed are missing is really the wisdom into their worth that comes from being a creature of God. Lastly, the "pride" that Jim Redmond had for his son Derek was really the wisdom to see what was more important than achieving the gold medal.

This chapter opened by claiming that the hinge upon which pride and wisdom swings is the question of how we understand our humanity. Pride is a distinctly human vice, where we ironically imagine ourselves more than human. Wisdom is the virtue of those who know and recognize the truth and understand its ultimate source to be in God, and understand their humanity in relation to God. Wisdom is a lofty virtue, preeminent among the cardinal excellences in both Greek and Christian traditions. Wisdom was present at creation according to Proverbs and John's Gospel, celebrated crown of Solomon, highest virtue in Plato's *Republic*, and the most divine human capacity according to Aristotle. Wisdom knows truth, and when acquired it binds the soul to truth with a strength that no dry intellectualism can attain. But wisdom, we might say, also knows the knower; it is self-aware. This is to say that wisdom does not abstract away one's empathetic insight into the human condition, but unites our rationality with our empathy.

Wisdom knows reality, and it knows it whole. Knowing something whole, however, does not mean knowing everything. Rather, it knows what it knows from the perspective of the whole—that is, it gets the big picture.

The wise are not smart at simply this or that thing, they orient the whole of their life to the good. In addition, as Socrates defended in his trial, wisdom ironically knows more than absolute knowledge because it knows its perpetual ignorance. The intimacy of wisdom and philosophic ignorance is only heightened in a Christian context where we seek to know God. For this reason, wisdom is neither science nor skill, neither certainty nor creed. Wisdom, above all, knows how to *live*, and to live is to always be on the way toward something. And thus, as Socrates demonstrated *after* he received the guilty verdict at his trial, and Bernard referenced in defense of humility as a virtue, wisdom knows how to die.

3

ON BEING GRACED
Sloth and Faith

There are people with the most extraordinary ability to transform everything
into a business operation, whose whole life is a business operation, who fall
in love and are married, hear a joke, and admire a work of art with the same
businesslike zeal with which they work at the office.[1]

—SØREN KIERKEGAARD

BECOMING VIRTUOUS TAKES WORK. But what kind of work exactly?
To better grasp the work required for cultivating virtue, it would be
helpful to consider the vice we think most opposed to work: sloth.

Without putting too fine a point on it, we can creatively imagine that
each of the seven deadly vices has had its own high points in human history, those times when the particular vice paid visit to an entire culture or
dined regularly with its highest leaders. When the vice of pride looks to
the past, it might swell with nostalgia as it considers the Roman Empire
a century before its fall, or 1938 Nazi Germany. Greed has certainly had
its heyday among the decadent nobility in eighteenth-century Europe or

1. Kierkegaard, *Either/Or*, 289.

in the company of the late twentieth-century dictators who have plagued Africa. But when the vice of sloth lounges in leisure and lazily leafs through the photo album of its travels over the centuries, which cultures would be pictured? Where has it thrived? Would we find any photos of twenty-first-century United States in its scrapbook?

In our culture that publicly denounces the couch potatoes among us, and that exports our national symbol of achievement and performance (Nike) across the globe, we might be surprised to find ourselves recounted in sloth's memoirs. We Americans can hold our heads high for keeping our citizens the busiest among the world's populations. By most statistics, Americans work more hours per week at their jobs than the citizens of any other nation around the world.[2] And when we add in all that we accomplish during our off hours including shopping, getting kids to their after-school activities, checking online for the latest news, Facebook, and email updates—well, we should all squeeze in a trip to the nearest caffeine fill-up station and take a quick break, secure in the knowledge that at least *this* vice has not gotten the best of us.

Before we congratulate ourselves on our industrious avoidance of sloth, however, we should clarify what we mean by the vice. While indeed sloth may slow one's work ethic or confine one to their Lazy-Boy and iPad for the weekend, increasing one's productivity might not counteract the real source of the vice. In fact, such efforts may miss the meaning of sloth altogether. As we shall see, incessant busyness often prevents the slothful from seeing their own vice, for like all virtues and vices, sloth is more complex than it first appears. And once we appreciate that complexity, we can see more clearly the distinct place sloth's opposing virtue, *faith*, has among the seven virtues, and in the life of the Christian.

When considering the virtue of faith, things are no less clear. For in some ways, faith is the virtue most difficult to fit into the list of seven. It is legitimate to ask at the outset, "Is faith actually a virtue?" In our first chapter, we asked whether pride was itself a vice. The question of faith's place among the virtues arises for a different reason. Certainly, faith is a praiseworthy character trait of Christians. Some may argue it is *the* defining character trait for Christians. And yet despite its primacy, it is not clear whether faith is a virtue *proper*. Why? Though it will take some time to unpack this, we can state the difficulty briefly: Christians hold that faith is a divine gift, and as a gift must function differently than a virtue acquired through habituation or learning. It must involve something distinct from human striving after an excellence like wisdom or habituating oneself to an excellence like

2. Schabner, "Americans Work More than Anyone."

temperance. In fact, it was on these points that the reformer Martin Luther vehemently critiqued Aristotle and his influence on Christian theology, and questioned the centrality of a virtue approach to Christian ethics. Luther's critique should not be taken lightly. As he would put it, faith is the result of grace and not merit, and virtue ethics look a lot like merit-based morality. Virtue takes work, and yet faith is a gift.

This difficulty is precisely why clarifying the meaning of sloth becomes so critical. As a pair, faith and sloth swing on a shared hinge. That hinge is the human capacity to be *receptive* to divine grace. It might seem as though the capacity to receive a gift requires nothing at all, and hence no "work." And yet, becoming receptive to the divine defines the Christian charater of all the virtues. So just as wisdom and pride grounded the virtues and vices in our human nature, so faith and sloth ground the virtues and vices in our graced nature. In the coming pages, we will clarify not only how faith can be a virtue, but how we Christians reimagined the virtues in light of the nature of faith.

SLOTH: FROM LAZINESS TO DESPAIR

Like any vice, sloth is a disposition to act in inferior and abhorrent ways, cultivated over time through habit, that prevents human flourishing and the person's attainment of a good life as a child of God. When it becomes an ingrained character trait that shapes our desires in a regular and consistent way, our poor decisions are truly effortless. They are "second nature" to us. These poor decisions contradict, and over time erode, our human person.

In the Christian tradition, sloth is a contemporary English word for the Latin *acedia*. To get at the root of sloth and its danger to our well-being, we must first work through several of its most apparent symptoms. In looking at two of these—laziness and despair—our goal is to get beyond these manifestations of the vice so that we may see more clearly what lies at its root. And so we should remember in our exploration that sloth and faith are not merely psychological states of mind but enduring and identifying moral dispositions of character. The difference is that whereas a psychological state is a biological pattern of our mental functioning, a moral disposition is the manner in which we as holistic persons are oriented (or not) toward God and neighbor. Psychology and morality are not independent of each other, but neither is one reducible to the other. Human flourishing, as we have noted, is not reducible to psychological health for the simple reason that we are more than our psyches. We are embodied spirits made in the image of our Creator, furnished with reason, possessing a heart that imagines its own good ends and is integrated with our organic, material being. Thus like all *deadly* sins, sloth brings death not merely to a set of positive feelings—for example, optimism, levity, presence—but to a *person* in all their rich complexity.

We begin with the most common connotation of sloth in our society: laziness. Many mistakenly assume this as the defining trait of *acedia*. If *acedia* were mere laziness, the obvious cure would entail staying active, and keeping oneself moving and occupied with the tasks of life so that the vice has nowhere to creep into our filled schedules. Idle hands are the devil's playground, right? The problem with those monks and desert fathers who first identified this vice, we might think, was that they didn't have enough to do! It is this mistaken assumption that can drive our frenetic twenty-first-century American lifestyles, where we work fifty- to sixty-hour weeks, run endless errands, exercise on our lunch breaks, or demand that our employees take no more than two weeks of vacation a year. Ironically, as those monks knew well, such efforts to avoid sloth can actually cultivate it even more.

Whether *acedia* is the same as laziness depends, of course, on *what kind of work* we think the slothful are avoiding. Too often, people confine laziness to the resistance toward productive work. Productive work certainly is one of the basic ways that we exercise our humanity and contribute to the sustained well-being of our community. Much of the moral imagination of modern culture has been shaped by our *economic* culture, which values individual work and productivity. Often, the American hope is that hard work will result in higher compensation, and that when society is just, those who have achieved great wealth have done so through their own individual effort and intelligence. In such a context, sloth denotes a form of laziness from such productive work and individual effort, and by extension a shirking of communal responsibility. The slothful, in this framework, do not work, or do not work enough, nor are they motivated to be productive or contribute economically to their family, company, institution, or society. In contrast to their industrious fellow citizens, the slothful remain languid and indolent.

Acedia, however, originally referred to something broader than the disdain for work in the worldly economy of production. It marked, rather, a spiritual despair and refusal to participate in the divine economy of grace. In its earliest conception among the dessert fathers, *acedia* manifested as a psychological state of melancholy, but its roots ran deeper as a form of despair engrained in the soul. That said, if sloth were mere melancholy, then the obvious cure would entail some self-esteem exercises, or diverting those dark feelings with the comforts of mindless entertainment. Again, we might assume that the problem with those thirteenth-century theologians was that they spent their days in dark libraries with little sun and no fun. That's why we twenty-first-century Americans think we have it made, given that we probably publish more self-help books than any other nation on earth and offer our citizens an endless array of cable channels and online diversions to perk us up.

The Evolution of a Vice

In her book, *Glittering Vices*, Rebecca DeYoung gives a helpful evolutionary history of the vice from the fourth to the fifteenth centuries. In the earliest description of the vice by fouth-century Egyptian desert father Evagrius Ponticus, *acedia* was one of the eight "deadly thoughts" marked by a weariness of the monk toward their own solitary religious commitment. Evagrius called it the noonday demon because it often afflicted his fellow monks during the middle of the day when one's morning energy and anticipation wane. Like all vices, sloth manifests itself through the most everyday of experiences and behaviors. Despite its seeming banality, sloth was one of the most frightening "demons" for these monks. According to DeYoung, monks were susceptible to being oppressed by the tedium of life, depressed at their spiritual calling, and were easily tempted to leave the heat of their cell for the entertainment of the city.[3] Consider Evagrius's description of the experience of *acedia*.

> First, [*acedia*] makes the sun appear sluggish and immobile, as if the day had fifty hours. Then he causes the monk continuously to look at the windows and forces him to step out of his cell and to gaze at the sun to see how far it still is from the ninth hour, and to look around, here and there, whether any of his brethren is near. Moreover, the demon sends him hatred against the place, against life itself, and against the work of his hands, and makes him think he has lost the love among his brethren and that there is none to comfort him. . . . He stirs the monk also to long for different places in which he can find easily what is necessary for his life and can carry on a much less toilsome and more expedient profession.[4]

Who among us is unacquainted with such an experience? Though the context of this description is that of a monastic desert father, the description speaks to many of us. Indeed, *acedia* is a depressed-like state that can

---

3. DeYoung, *Glittering Vices*, 97.
4. Evagrius, cited in Ferguson, *Melancholy*, 9.

afflict us during the middle of the day, the middle of the week, or the middle of life—where task becomes tedium, vocation becomes vacuous, ritual becomes rut, and where we can no longer experience the vitality of life or the goodness of love. *Acedia* afflicts one with the mundane wherein the everydayness of our lives bears down upon our once-impassioned souls as if to remind us, "Vanity of vanities! All is vanity. What do people gain from all the toil at which they toil under the sun? . . . All things are wearisome; more than one can express; the eye is not satisfied with seeing, or the ear filled with hearing. What has been is what will be, and what has been done is what will be done; there is nothing new under the sun" (Eccl 1:2–3, 8–9).

A later interpretation of *acedia* was articulated by Cassian, who lived in a communal monastery. For Cassian, *acedia* entailed a lack of desire to participate in the community work and worship. Because it was more than a spiritual deficiency with regard to one's love of God, and affected one's love of neighbor as well, *acedia* became all the more shameful within the moral community.

This view of a spiritual and moral despair was expanded in the thirteenth century by Thomas Aquinas, who sees *acedia* targeted against the virtue of love (*caritas*). This expanded the intentionality of *acedia* to include more than one's direct relationship to God or ecclesial community. It interfered with one's reception of and participation in the gift of God's love and our own virtuous journey toward friendship with God. Overcome by such sorrow, Aquinas notes that sloth is more than weariness from work but a despair over that which is good. He writes in the *Summa Theologia* that sloth "is an oppressive sorrow, which, to wit, so weighs upon man's mind, that he wants to do nothing; thus acid things are also cold. Hence sloth implies a certain weariness of work . . . from the definition of some who say that sloth is a "sluggishness of the mind which neglects to being good."[5]

In the evolution of the concept of *acedia*, it become more associated with what Thomas would call the effects of its sorrow ("drawing away from good deeds") than the source of its sorrow ("sorrow about spiritual goods.") This emphasis on the effects of sloth would only increase after the Protestant Reformation, when the meaning of sloth became applied broadly enough that it could be seen as laziness in any form of human work. This more universal application of the vice not only fit the trajectory Aquinas set in motion, but also the novel manner in which Martin Luther saw human vocational callings previously seen as secular to be legitimate Christian callings.

5. Aquinas, *Summa Theologica*, II.II.35.1

From Sloth to Faith

Sloth's despair marks an ingrained incapacity to receive grace and its laziness marks an ingrained incapacity to act in the world as a response to grace. "[*Acedia*] is a profound withdrawal into self. Action is no longer perceived as a gift to oneself, as the response to a prior love that calls us, enables our action, and makes it possible." For these reasons, I think, Aquinas described it in truly frightening language, "Despair is not the most serious sin, but it is the most dangerous of all . . . it is a state of being that is proper to the damned."[6] For as John Chrysostom said, "It is not so much sin as despair which casts us into hell."[7]

In the previous chapter we noted that pride foolishly claims oneself as the source of goodness. Sloth, on the other hand, despairs because it denies that goodness could ever be given to oneself. Neither of these vices allows the gifts from the divine giver to be received with gratitude. *Acedia* is thus referred to as a "perverted humility," where one denies the greatness bestowed on humanity by a loving God. Whereas pride minimizes the source of the image (namely God) for the sake of bolstering the self, sloth minimizes the image itself by despairing that we actually could not be an image of the divine. Josef Pieper writes that "*Acedia* is, in the last analysis, a 'destatio boni divini,' with the monstrous result that upon reflection, man expressly wishes that God had not ennobled him but had 'left him in peace.'"[8]

When the vice of sloth takes root in the soul, like pride, it fixates the individual on one's own self and away from God. Whereas pride wrongly considers the self its own salvation and source of triumph, sloth burdens the person with one's own emptiness, leaving him or her with the sheer banality of everyday life. Contemporary Christian writer Kathleen Norris writes in her recent book, *Acedia and Me*, that once *acedia* takes hold, "even if she knows what is spiritually good for her, she is tempted to deny that her inner beauty and spiritual strength are at her disposal, as gifts from God."[9]

In the end, sloth prevents us from being receptive to the gifts of God, of living into those gifts, and thus working for others in light of those gifts. To limit sloth to the resistance to productive work is to be caught in a world that defines happiness, accomplishment, and merit in terms of productive work. This is the mark of an age of secularization that accomplishes amazing things but has no receptivity to the grace of God. Something has to fill the

---

6. Aquinas, *Summa Theologia*, II-II.20.1.3

7. Chysostom, *Commentary on Matthew 27*, cited in Pieper, *Faith, Hope, Love*, 117.

8. Pieper, *Faith Hope and Love*, 119.

9. Norris, *Acedia and Me*, 21.

void left by one's denial of the graced dignity of being human, and thus we work incessantly to prop up our own industrial worth. Pieper concludes that "*Acedia* is the signature of every age that seeks, in its despair, to shake off the obligations of that nobility of being that is conferred by Christianity and so, in its despair, to deny its true self."[10]

We now turn from vice to virtue. Keeping in mind the above descriptions of sloth as both laziness and despair, we can now understand faith as its corrective. The ground has already been laid with our conclusions about sloth as a despairing disposition toward divine grace. While suggestive of where to go next, our examination so far has been from the standpoint of the vice alone. Teaching someone how to avoid a vice does not yet guide that person toward virtue. Admitting to the problem may be the first step toward the cure, but it is not yet the cure. To accomplish this later task, we must now bring faith into view. As we have noted, faith and sloth swing on a shared hinge. That hinge is the human capacity to be *receptive* to and *participate* in divine grace. In order to see how this capacity counters the various manifestations of sloth, we need to examine how the communal and individual practices of faith are redemptive to the slothful.

In the introduction I described a moral virtue as a settled disposition of a person to act in excellent and praiseworthy ways, cultivated over time through habit. Here we consider faith as a virtue, and not, strictly as doctrinal or theological ascent or belief. Faith as a virtue is something lived, not simply believed; it is a consistent and enduring quality of one's character, not only knowledge of orthodoxy. As a virtue, though, faith has its own distinct character in the Christian tradition. Faith is a *theological* virtue; that is, it has its origins explicitly in a divine gift and not human nature as such. This poses some problems for understanding the virtues as cultivated forms of human excellence. Medieval theologians debated whether all, some, or none of the virtues required the infusion of divine grace. Regardless of where specific thinkers came down on this issue, most agreed that there were three distinctly theological virtues: faith, hope, and love. As Paul writes in his letter to the Ephesians, "For by grace you have been saved through faith, and this is not your own doing; it is a gift of God—not the result of merit, so that no one may boast" (2:8–9).

Faith in the Body of Christ: Leisure and Liturgy

To understand how exploring faith helps us specifically against sloth, let us first return to the world of economic work, and see how we might move

10. Pieper, *Faith Hope and Love*, 122.

from here to an appreciation of faith. To make this journey, we need to begin with something often considered the opposite of work, namely *leisure*. Yale University political scientist Robert Lane argues in his recent book *The Loss of Happiness in Market Democracies* that since 1960, there has been an inverse relationship between an increasing GNP among developed countries and a host of metrics indicating happiness, satisfaction, or overall contentment with life. In general, as a nation's gross national product increases, the percentage of citizens who report being "very happy" decreases. The analysis of this trend is more complex than this simple summary, but Lane argues throughout the book that despite an increase in economic productivity, there has been

> a postwar decline in the United States in people who report themselves as happy, a rising tide in all advanced societies of clinical depression and dysphoria (especially among the young), increasing distrust of each other and of political and other institutions, declining belief that the lot of the average man is getting better, a tragic erosion of family solidarity and community integration together with an apparent decline in warm, intimate relationships among friends.[11]

This social phenomenon can be somewhat appreciated through the theological framework of attempting to counter the spiritual despair of sloth with only industriousness. This is not to say that people had more faith when our country was poorer, but rather to indicate the difficulties industriousness can pose to spiritual well being. Consider what it means to work too much. On the one hand, this may mean putting in too many hours, where one is *at work* too much and *at home* too little. For some, this work/life imbalance is a very real problem. If being human entails more than being a worker, then limiting the amount of time available to cultivate other non-work human capacities will impede being virtuous. On the other hand, a different problem of "working too much" results from not being able to escape a *worklike attitude* toward the rest of life. Whether one is "at work" or not, those afflicted with this problem bring their work with them always. Consider again the quote by Søren Kierkegaard with which I opened this chapter, in which he critiques the effect of Denmark's newly modernized economy on the Danish people. "There are people with the most extraordinary ability to transform everything into a business operation, whose whole life is a business operation, who fall in love and are married, hear a joke, and

---

11. Lane, *Loss of Happiness in Market Democracies*, 3.

admire a work of art with the same businesslike zeal with which they work at the office"[12]

What does this attitude entail, and why is it so problematic? Such zeal entails the thrill and energy of working on a project, setting goals, meeting deadlines, marking off calendars, checking off tasks, fixing problems, finishing the production, or closing the sale. With regard to our anthropology, the center of this passion is the *will*—that which exerts one's power to tasks and commits to completing them with vigor and on deadline. Kierkegaard's critique is not that a "businesslike zeal" interferes with work, but rather that it is not a disposition one should carry into personal relationships, worship, leisure, aesthetic appreciation, or even humor. We know people like this, or experience it in ourselves perhaps. In such a mindset, our children, spouses, and friends become like colleagues. The family dinner table mirrors a committee meeting. We negotiate and haggle with our roommates or spouses to maximize the success of the home office. Everything becomes a problem to be solved or a project to be managed. Our childrens' anxieties, illnesses, and sibling rivalries become setbacks that need a solution strategy. If we are lucky, our loved one's try to pull us out of this: "Can't you just leave work at work?!"

If sloth entails the corruption of our attitude toward human labor, *it* may be just as responsible for laziness as it is for busyness. Tim Kreider wrote in a recent commentary in the *New York Times*, "Busyness serves as a kind of existential reassurance, a hedge against emptiness; obviously your life cannot possibly be silly or trivial or meaningless if you are so busy, completely booked, in demand every hour of the day."[13]

In one of the more important philosophy books of the twentieth century, *Leisure as the Basis of Culture,* Josef Pieper critically examines the demise of meaningful leisure in contemporary society. He argues that we live increasingly in a "totalitarian work state." Our society is not totalitarian in its political organization, nor does American work culture mimic the centralized economies of twentieth-century communism. Rather, he argues, we have become a society where *work defines life*. Moreover, this totalization of work life not only translates into the number of hours we work, but more significantly, in how we think about non-work. In a short summary of these ideas in the essay "Work, Spare Time, and Leisure," Pieper claims that when our lives become defined by the single pole of work, we reduce leisure to mere "free time" or "time when we are not working," or "time to rejuvenate

---

12. Kierkegaard, *Either/Or*, 289.
13. Kreider, "The 'Busy' Trap," para. 6.

for more work."[14] Our evenings or weekends become merely time to "decompress" or "veg out" or "recharge."

Leisure, according to Pieper, used to mean a time of its own, the experience of which was the very goal of work. Lest you think that Pieper is arguing simply for more three-day weekends or a thirty-seven-hour workweek, consider how he distinguishes "leisure" from "free time." Pieper argues that genuine leisure allows one to participate in the contemplation of eternal and divine things, the gifts of God, and the tangible and festive celebrations of worship and feast days that open our spirits to such divine gratuity. Whether these activities include the intentional contemplation done in prayer, philosophical thinking, or theological reflection, or in the implicit activities of artistic creation and accompanying wonder over the natural world, or in meaningful conversation over shared meals with the friends or family in one's community, leisure was definitively not work. At the same time, leisure was also not defined negatively as "non-work." Leisure marks those activities that are *meaningful in themselves*, and not aimed toward some pragmatic or economic end. It possesses its own significance, which is at root *the practiced gratitude for existence*.

> An activity which is meaningful in itself, first, cannot be accomplished except with an attitude of receptive openness and attentive silence—which, indeed, is the exact opposite of the worker's attitude marked by concentrated exertion. One of the fundamental human experiences is the realization that the truly great and uplifting things in life come about perhaps not without our own efforts but nonetheless not though those efforts. Rather, we will obtain them only if we accept them as free gifts.[15]

In our discernment on how faith might correct sloth, we have our first clue here. Sloth interferes not simply with the activities for productive work, but more fundamentally with those activities that are meaningful in themselves. Those activities that are meaningful in themselves build up love of God and love of neighbor. Such activities don't just get us away from work—which sleeping in on Saturday would—but actually engage something essential to being human. These activities involve a receptivity to the gifts of God, and are not dependent solely on our own efforts.

Lest Pieper's description of leisure seem too broad or open-ended, he offers a second, and more concrete, condition for leisure: the ability to celebrate a feast. This requires more than a few days off of work. Rather, this requires a person's "willing acceptance of the ultimate truth, in spite

14. Pieper, "Work, Spare Time, and Leisure," 17.
15. Ibid., 25.

of the world's riddles, even when this truth is beheld through the veil of our own tears; it includes man's awareness of being in harmony with these fundamental realities and surrounded by them."[16] We are each to cultivate the capacity to celebrate life by connecting our rituals—worship, common meals, conversations—to the ultimate truth beyond us. That truth requires that we trust that our life here on earth is not meaningless, but grounded in reality. As such, the meaningfulness of our lives is not something completely dependent on our exertion or manufactured culture, as creative as that may be. The idol that humanity alone creates the purposes for which we exist feeds the hidden anxiety behind our obsession with work. Learning the practiced gratitude of existence, and connecting that to our communal rituals of worship, meals, and conversations is a corrective to both sloth and the errant avoidance of sloth found in busyness. Such a practice is intimately connected to faith *as a virtue*.

As the church, we resist sloth in the cultivation of faith through the practices of worship and Sabbath keeping. Such rituals offer a third way to break through alternatives of either productive work or "free time." The English word "liturgy" comes from the Greek work *leitourgia* and means literally "the work of the people." But this Sabbath work is not the economic production of the workweek, but rather the common activity of a people that come together to proclaim, celebrate, and be consecrated in their faith. The rituals and liturgies of our Sabbath worship engage our ability to celebrate a feast, the most obvious symbolic enactment being the Eucharist itself.

The cultivation of any virtue requires work. Its requires practice, habituation, mindfulness, and effort. The soul-forming work of the community of faith is the "work of the people" practiced in the liturgies of one's church, which give us the perspective from which to enter our individual vocations. Honoring the Sabbath is indeed one of the activities associated with the virtue of faith. Indeed, Aquinas considered sloth to be the vice that breaks the third commandment. Honoring the Sabbath gives honor to God for God's own generosity, thus cultivating our ability to be receptive to the grace of God. This is the fundamental work of faith that counters the despair and laziness of sloth.

Faith and Individual Character: Receptivity and Gratitude

Faith shapes the virtuous character of the church by situating the practices of the people of God in the cycle of God's generosity and our gratitude. As a

16. Ibid, 26.

virtue, faith also defines the individual members within the body of Christ and becomes manifest as a virtue cultivated within the person.

As a pairing of character traits in the individual, sloth and faith lie on the opposite end of the spectrum from pride and wisdom. Pride and wisdom are the perversion and ennobling of our *striving* after goodness and truth; sloth and faith, on the other hand, are the perversion and ennobling of our *receptivity* to goodness and truth. Faith is thus fundamentally the virtue whereby, paradoxically, we excel in our dependence on God.

Faith, of course, involves *recognizing* a fundamental truth about God and our relationships to God, whether this be expressed in a confession of faith like the Apostles' Creed, the words of John 3:16, or in the gospel as preached in one's local community of faith. We often think of faith as a form of belief, or an individual's epistemic assent to an idea or truth claim. "I believe in God the Father, maker of heaven and earth. And in Jesus Christ, his only son, . . . I believe in the Holy Spirit, the holy catholic church . . ." Christians, at times, focus on faith as an intellectual assent to a truth, and a willful decision to embrace that truth. Such a view animates how many think of conversion as a onetime decision of faith, as distinct from an ongoing call to personal and communal growth. The recognition/decision framework for faith, however, misses something more radical about the character of this virtue: faith originates in a gift.

To those of us in denominations stemming from Lutheranism, the language of faith as gift sinks deep into our theological imagination. Certainly the idea of faith as gift is universal to the Christian church, but Luther so consistently reflected on grace, gift, and gratitude that these became the "cardinal concepts of his theology."[17] Luther noted that faith is a divine gift that must to be received by us *continuously*, thus reflecting the *virtuous* character of faith that is cultivated over time through habit. Faith is more than *assent to belief* in God, it is an ongoing, trusting activity. Luther notes that the response to receiving this gift can only be *gratitude*, and thus just as faith is given continuously, so faith must continuously respond with gratitude. In his *Lectures on Romans*, Luther reflects on ingratitude and considers it one of the most hostile attitudes toward God. "Now let us look at the order and the various levels of perdition. The first level is ingratitude, or the omission of gratitude. . . . . [Where one] takes pleasure in things received, as if they were not received at all, and leaves the Giver out of consideration."[18] Luther continues by noting how faith understood as gratitude is the foundation of the virtuous life. In gratitude, the person retains the love of God in their

17. Luther, *What Luther Said*, 603.
18. Luther, *Works*, 31:159.

heart. In his recent book *Free of Charge*, theologian Miroslav Volf gets to the heart of these ideas by claiming that *faith is the way by which we as receivers relate appropriately to God as giver*. "God's gifts oblige us first to a posture of receptivity. Rather than wanting to earn God's gifts or receive them in return for some favor, we should see ourselves as who we truly are, namely receivers and receivers only. We do that by relating to God in faith."[19]

Faith recognizes the graced character of one's life and breath, a breath that continues even after we suffer or participate in loss, tragedy, or betrayal. Sloth denies us the possibilities for goodness offered by our sustained life. The slothful would rather mire in the stubborn darkness of their souls.

Faith also entails being receptive to forgiveness. That is, faith enables us to receive a gift we not only did not merit, but actively refused before. Faith receives the forgiving embrace of Christ and the neighbor who I have wronged. This is why faith becomes the foundation of a relationship to the divine: it confesses God's generous goodness and forgiveness and responds with gratitude by furthering that goodness in the world. Indeed, what else could ground a finite creature's relationship to a loving Creator?

In Aristotle's classic analysis of friendship in the *Nicomachean Ethics*, he considers the difficulty in navigating a friendship with someone who is truly superior to you whether in intelligence, virtue, or wealth. If friendships are supposed to be reciprocal, how could the inferior of the two reciprocate anything worthwhile to the superior? I can't match my rich friends' wealth, or my brilliant friends' intelligence, or my virtuous friends' excellence of character. Aristotle notes that in such situations, the inferior can give the superior something, namely *honor*. In the Christian context, where some imagine a friendship between us and God, we honor the divine by being first and foremost gracious recipients of God's goodness. But this gratitude is not a gift given *in return* for the gift. If it were, the transaction would be finished, the cycle of exchange complete. Rather, the cycle of grace and gratitude fosters an ongoing relationship. Luther claims that grace must be given *continuously to* us; and that faith is one of those divine gifts that is never exhausted.

In the end, faith has its own kind of work. Luther saw this when he wrote, "Do not think lightly of faith. It is a work that is of all works the most excellent and the most difficult. Through it alone you will be saved, even though you were obliged to do without all other works. For it is the work of God, not of man."[20] The work of faith is akin to the work of the people in the liturgy on the Sabbath. The work of faith is not like the work of striving after

19. Volf, *Free of Charge*, 42.
20. Luther, *Babylonian Captivity*, 224.

wisdom, nor the productive work of strenuously manipulating creation to bear fruit. Its most radical work is not recognition and decision either, but first and foremost receptivity and gratitude. Faith is an activity characterized by receptivity and participation in the cycle of gift and gratitude that a gracious God makes possible through the saving work of Christ.

CONCLUSION

We began this chapter by noting that becoming virtuous requires work, and then asked about the kind of work that faith might require. The particular difficulty that faith poses within the framework of Christian virtues is that it depends constantly and explicitly on a divine gift. This is why a theological virtue like faith requires that we rethink the overall character of any virtue.

Sloth is an ingrained aversion to the work of faith, and by extension the work of doing good in the world. This is why faith, and not busyness and constant activity, is the corrective to sloth. Sloth is precisely a kind of spiritual despair that results from the incapacity to receive the good gift of divine grace; faith, in its receptivity to God's activity, enables a life pleasing to God as a response. American-style industriousness is not the solution to sloth, because the problem was not originally not doing enough, but of not knowing how to receive enough with gratitude. To the extent that we resist the most basic disposition of gratitude, Luther would say, we become overcome with the empty weight of our own selves.

We asked whether faith should be considered a virtue proper? While faith never loses its essential character as a divine gift, once it is given by God to the receptive heart, it functions as a virtue because the person is disposed to act in excellent and praiseworthy ways over time through the hard work of habituation. In the work of sanctification, faith takes root in the soul.

4

ON BEING TEMPORAL
Greed and Hope

It's a mystery to me
We have a greed with which we have agreed
And you think you have to want more than you need
Until you have it all, you won't be free

—EDDIE VEDDER, "SOCIETY"

GREED IS A TIMELY vice.
The daily financial news reminds us of our collective struggle to regain our bearings after years of greed in the banking industry. When we heard of the major banks receiving bailouts after years of excess, and then giving billions in bonuses to their top executives, we staggered to grasp a situation out of control. When we read stories of these same bank executives securing their own private stock of H1N1 vaccines before other target populations were allowed access to immunization, we strained to understand the behavior of those for whom money can buy anything.

Greed would seem to be one of the more straightforward vices. It tends to be a rather public vice as well. "Conspicuous consumption," my father would call it. Its true, greed is often conspicuous and thus appears to be a more obvious vice than many others. In this book, however, we seek a more nuanced analysis made available by discovering the "hinges" upon which pairs of virtues and vices swing. As we noted in earlier chapters, the hinge upon which wisdom and pride swing is the meaning of humanity as such— pride distorts our view of humanity, wisdom sees it clearly. For sloth and faith, the hinge was our receptivity to divine grace—sloth refuses to receive grace while faith embraces the divine gift.

In this chapter, we look for the hinge upon which greed and hope swing. What we discover in this odd pairing is that the hinge upon which they swing is *time*, or more precisely, the manner in which human beings live into time. In this light, I contend that greed viciously attempts to control *time*, and that this desire is more fundamental than the desire for material stuff, money, or power. I do not dismiss the reality of unrestrained materialistic desires that many embrace, nor the tradition of defining greed as excessive material attachment. Rather, I will argue that excessive material acquisitiveness is a manifestation of our vicious disposition toward human temporality. Thus in contrast to greed, hope is the virtuous way we live into our human temporality.

But how do I get to this claim? Along our journey toward this insight, we will meet a host of characters from the absurdly wealthy Lloyd Blankfein of Goldman Sachs, to a landowning peasant in nineteenth-century Russia, to the utterly austere fourth-century desert fathers. Somehow, greed tempts each of these characters. So, lest we get too comfortable scapegoating the Blankfeins of this world, the desert fathers will challenge our self-assurance in our own presumably temperate ways.

THE EASY TARGET

Let us first bring to mind a familiar picture of the vice. In its traditional definition, greed is *excessive acquisitiveness*.

I noted in the first chapter that virtues are dispositions to act in excellent ways deemed praiseworthy by a moral community that encourages such excellences. We review again several conditions for the realization of a virtue within an individual. Virtues require

- a social group with which its members identify;

- exemplars of the virtue within the community that others desire to imitate;

- habituated practices that aim toward goods meaningful to the community;

- a *telos* that the members work toward in common.

As a mirror to the virtues, our vices are no less communal in character. They too are strengthened by a social group, exemplars, and habits that direct individual desire toward some *telos*, albeit a distorted one.

To illustrate these elements, we take a brief look at Lloyd Blankfein, the CEO of the global investment banking and securities firm Goldman Sachs. Blankfein became one of the poster boys for the latest wave of greed in the investment banking industry. Along with a host of other financial institutions, Goldman played a part in the meltdown that almost leveled the global financial system. It lent too much money, lost too much money, and took bailout cash from Washington. In a telling interview with John Arlidge printed in the *Sunday Times*,[1] we can see the character of this vice and the surrounding culture at Goldman Sachs. The interview is helpful to consider not only because it provides an all too easy target of the vice, but more importantly, because it indicates key elements operative within the manifestation of the vice. Arlidge notes that Blankfein starts the interview with a little humility:

> "I know I could slit my wrists and people would cheer," he says. But then, he slowly begins to argue the case for modern banking. "We're very important," he says, abandoning self-flagellation. "We help companies to grow by helping them to raise capital. Companies that grow create wealth. This, in turn, allows people to have jobs that create more growth and more wealth. It's a virtuous cycle."

Heroes such as Blankfein, and he is considered heroic by many, require a community to bequeath them such honor. That community is Goldman Sachs, which perhaps more than any other bank has an identifiable culture about it.[2] Goldman Sachs attracts and hires only those individuals with a wealth of intellectual talent and ambitious energy to convert that intellectual capital into monetary gain. Arlidge asks an important question in his commentary.

> What makes people who are bright enough to do anything they want put up with the days-into-nights-into-days working and the dorkish corporate groupthink? There's the money, of course. Goldman Sachs isn't nicknamed "Goldmine Sachs" for nothing. There's so much of the stuff sloshing around that in an average

1. Arlidge, "I'm Doing 'God's Work,'" para. 8.
2. For another take on the "culture" at Goldman Sachs, see Smith, "Why I Am Leaving Goldman Sachs."

year a good investment banking partner will make $3.5m, a
good trading partner $7–10m and a management committee
member $15–25m. . . . One former Goldman banker describes
the culture as "completely money-obsessed." "I was like a donkey driven forward by the biggest, juiciest carrot I could imagine. Money is the way you define your success. There's always
room—need—for more. If you are not getting a bigger house
or a bigger boat, you're falling behind. It's an addiction." Addiction is a word Sherwood uses, too. He should know. He's on his
second multi-million-pound super-yacht.[3]

This depiction of greed is familiar and fits with the notion that the vice
is an obsession with acquisition, whether it is of boats, houses, or just plain
cash. Arlidge, however, notes another component of the psychology operative within the culture of greed.

But there's another powerful motivator [to getting brilliant
graduates to work endless hours at Goldman Sachs]: *doubt*.
There may be arrogance at 85 Broad Street—behind closed
doors, Blankfein likes to joke (but not really) that he has "attained perfection"—but behind the bravado, Goldmanites,
curiously, question their ability. "There is a deep and constant
paranoia about everything we do," says Sherwood. "It applies to
an individual's performance and the prospects for the firm as a
whole. Insecurity is hard-wired into the system."[4]

Doubt persistently troubles the avaricious. The greedy are never at
peace with their holdings. This aspect of greed is not the case with all vices.
Pride, for example, in its full flowering, does not manifest such unsettled-
ness. Quite the contrary, pride's self-obsession is often oblivious to such
anxiety. That obliviousness is one of its chief problems. Sloth also fails to
display such fundamental apprehension as it drifts into its own numbing
melancholy. But greed, like its close relatives gluttony and envy, operates
under a perpetual disquiet.

A final element of a virtuous or vicious community is its *telos*, the goal
that drives its actions and choices. Reading the interview with Blankfein, it
would be good to nuance his earlier claim that Goldman Sachs has a social
purpose. Goldman Sachs indeed plays a role in the organization of wealth
that contributes to the economic functionings of the global market. That
role is the one seen from the perspective of the world outside Goldman
Sachs. It does not, however, describe the final end internal to the financial

3. Arlidge, "I'm Doing 'God's Work.'"
4. Ibid.

firm. In the conclusion to his interview, Arlidge indicates the *telos* Blankfein
ascribes to the firm and his likeminded associates.

> For Blankfein, in the end, it all comes down to one thing: find-
> ing the best, fastest, and safest way to make money with money,
> then make some more money, with money on top. . . . I ask him
> the question that, in these troubled times, you'd think anyone
> . . . would pause before answering. . . . "Is it possible to make too
> much money?"
>
> "Is it possible to have too much ambition? Is it possible to
> be too successful?" Blankfein shoots back. "I don't want people
> in this firm to think that they have accomplished as much for
> themselves as they can and go on vacation. As the guardian of
> the interests of the shareholders and, by the way, for the pur-
> poses of society, I'd like them to continue to do what they are
> doing. I don't want to put a cap on their ambition. It's hard for
> me to argue for a cap on their compensation."
>
> So, it's business as usual, then, regardless of whether it makes
> most people howl at the moon with rage? Goldman Sachs, this
> pillar of the free market, breeder of super-citizens, object of
> envy and awe will go on raking it in, getting richer than God?
> An impish grin spreads across Blankfein's face. Call him a fat cat
> who mocks the public. Call him wicked. Call him what you will.
> He is, he says, just a banker "doing God's work."

In this community with its practiced habits and well-defined *telos*, Blankfein functions as the virtuous exemplar. In his most successful year, 2007,
the Goldman Sachs boss was compensated $68 million, a record for any
Wall Street CEO.

Blankfein and the culture at Goldman Sachs serve as easy targets, and
I don't mean to present my analysis of this interview as a comprehensive
picture of Blankfein or Goldman Sachs. Rather I use it because it succinctly
shows the elements that make up greed as *excessive acquisition*. After all, this
latest round of greed writ large in the banking industry has descended upon
us just after our recovery from greed in the energy industry exemplified
by Enron, which came just after the illness of "infectious greed" that Alan
Greenspan diagnosed during the 1990s Wall Street and dot-coms surge,
which, of course, has been repeated throughout history. If greed is a vice
that is never satisfied, cultures that suffer its ill effects never seem to learn
their lesson either.

From Excessive Acquisitions to Excessive Attachments

In the movie *Wall Street*, actor Michael Douglass, playing a highly success-ful investor, delivered one of the more famous movie speeches: "The point is, ladies and gentleman, that greed—for lack of a better word—is good. Greed is right. Greed works. Greed clarifies, cuts through, and captures the es-sence of the evolutionary spirit. Greed, in all of its forms—greed for life, for money, for love, knowledge—has marked the upward surge of mankind." The key phrase in Gecko's otherwise rhetorically brilliant speech is "for lack of a better word." Gecko's linguistic imagination is limited by his moral imagination.[5] Indeed, applying the concept of greed to objects as diverse as money, love, and knowledge is a misnomer. But wherein lies the problem?

Virtues and vices are the orderings and dis-orderings of our desires, which have been habituated over time by a series of wise or poor choices or encouraged by good or bad mentors. Unlike a worldview present in certain kinds of Buddhism, which admonishes the extinction of all desire from the human soul, Western culture and Christianity by and large encourage cultivating our desires. That said, our appetites do not cultivate themselves toward virtue. As Aristotle notes, moral virtues are not acquired by nature, though a properly nurtured soul acts in accordance with its nature. Virtues must be taught, habituated, and enculturated in the person over time. And so if we as Christians are to cultivate our desires, and arouse those that are good, the problem with greed must be clarified. For example, can one actu-ally have a greed for love?

Like all the vices in their infancy within the human heart, greed is subtle in its mimicry of otherwise good desires. Consider, for example, the other vices as they arise innocuously in the soul. In its youth, pride imper-sonates self-respect and often seems to be a necessary virtue for someone seeking to overcome unjust humiliation or marginalization. Sloth, likewise, also eases its way into the habits of the heart when we begin to misapply the proper meaning of Sabbath. And as we shall see with lust, when it stirs in the embodied soul of the otherwise temperate person, it can at first seem like merely a welcomed feeling of human vitality. When we examine the disorders of greed, we see that it too masquerades as an otherwise good desire that includes our attachment to place, earthly goods, and even family and friends.

---

5. One could also debate his claim that greed captures the essence of the evolution-ary spirit, since among higher order mammals, altruism seems as likely, if not more so, to produce an evolutionary advantage as egoism. The question of the evolutionary development of altruism has been debated since Darwin himself, and currently engages philosophical biologists and psychologists including E.O. Wilson and Steven Pinker.

According to Aquinas, avarice takes two forms. First, it is a vice in so far as it effectively steals goods from others for one's selfish acquisitions. Such an outward vice is countered by justice. In its second form, however, greed entails an inner excessive attachment to something. In this regard, greed appears to belong in the triad of vices that include gluttony and lust. As gluttony is to food, and lust is to sex, so greed is to wealth. All are distinguished by the distortion of the desired through an excessive attachment to the desire itself, which results in an activity akin to frenetic consumption that reduces the desired to a means of immediate self-satisfaction. Greed distorts our attachments because it demotes everything it desires to something that can be merely bought, possessed, owned, or controlled.

Those goods that properly can be possessed, owned, and controlled—of which money is the quintessence—offer limited satisfaction unless they are used for the sake of goods that promote our higher order-desires, for example, love, family, sense of place, church, and God. This unfettered desire for the possession of *things* is a most conspicuous characteristic, evidenced in our example of Goldman Sachs. Greed for money is a distorted desire, but its object is precisely the kind of thing that can be so desired. Gecko's praise of the "greed for love" is not only a distorted desire, but a distortion of the nature of the *object* of desire itself. "Greed for love" is thus both doubly wrongheaded, and thus also doubly impossible to satisfy. The only solution for this lack of fulfillment is to make acquisition itself the highest good.

In the biblical book of Genesis, Abram and Lot display the gulf between the virtue and vice with regard to the attachment to wealth. In the story, both are to be granted land. Having been given the first choice of land, Lot greedily seizes the best for himself, leaving the desert to an uncomplaining Abram. Abram trusts that the Lord will provide, though his present dwelling on a tired and thirsty ground might indicate otherwise. Lot, however, becomes so attached to the pleasantries and luxuries of the good life in Sodom that even when his and his family's lives are in jeopardy, angels themselves have to drag him away. Rebecca DeYoung notes in her book *Glittering Vices*, "As with any habit, [greed] depends on actions wearing a groove or pattern in the longings of our hearts."[6] Accustomed to the entrapments of a decadent lifestyle, Lot's attachments are not easily wrested free from his engrained habits of consumption. Once it takes root in the human soul, greed prevents even an otherwise holy person from being free for the Lord.

The outward symptoms of greed belie their inward motivation. Along with excessive acquisitiveness and attachment, it should be remembered

6. DeYoung, *Glittering Vices*, 101.

that greed is accompanied by a fundamental *anxiety*. We saw this in the culture at Goldman Sachs. Examining this anxiety more closely offers a deeper understanding of the vice and a more enduring corrective to it.

From Attachment to Ambition: "A Thousand Rubles a Day"

Alongside the monumental literary works of Leo Tolstoy one may find a small gem titled "How Much Land Does a Man Need?" This short story deftly illustrates a host of human experiences ranging from poverty to ambition. It also brings in an essential element of greed oft overlooked in most contemporary accounts of the vice: time. At the start of the story, the Russian peasant Pahom listens to an argument between his two grown daughters over which life is preferable: a life of wealth in the city or of simplicity in the country. The younger peasant sister defends her present life,

> We may live roughly, but at least we are free from anxiety. You live in better style than we do, but though you often earn more than you need, you are very likely to lose all you have. You know the proverb, 'Loss and gain are brothers twain.' Though a peasant's life is not a fat one, it is a long one. We shall never grow rich, but we shall always have enough to eat.[7]

Proud of his youngest daughter, Pahom boasts, "It is perfectly true, busy as we are from childhood tilling mother earth, we peasants have *no time* to let any nonsense settle in our heads. Our only trouble is that we haven't land enough. If I had plenty of land, I shouldn't fear the Devil himself!" All the while, the Devil himself listens in and decides to challenge Pahom's claim. The narrative that ensues is a reversal of the biblical story of Job. Over the course of many years, the Devil cultivates ambition and greed in Pahom through his singular desire to have *enough* land, by giving Pahom opportunity after opportunity to expand his landholdings. Eventually, Pahom learns of a remote region in Russia with the richest, virgin topsoil, owned by a simple nomadic people, who will grant great areas of land to gift-bearing visitors seeking to settle in their region. Pahom is advised by the Devil, disguised as a traveling merchant, on the necessary customs to observe in order to garner favor with the tribes people.

After successfully earning their trust, the Chief of the Bashins offers Pahom as much land as he desires for a single price, "one thousand rubles a day." Pahom does not understand. "A day? What measure is that? How many acres would that be?"

7. Tolstoy, "How Much Land Does a Man Need?"

"We do not know how to reckon it out," said the Chief. "We sell it by the day. As much as you can go round on your feet in a day is yours, and the price is one thousand rubles a day."

Pahom was surprised. "But in a day you can get round a large tract of land," he said.

The Chief laughed. "It will all be yours!" said he. "But there is one condition: If you don't return on the same day to the spot whence you started, your money is lost."

Spoiler alert: in the climactic final scene Pahom rises early in the morning, meets with the chief and tribesmen, and sets out on his journey of acquisition. His whole life is played out in this single day. He begins with the thoughts of a farmer, rather temperate but energetic, but in the course of time his desire for gain overtakes him to the point that he has walked too far from his original starting point. With the sun beginning to set, his legs fatigued and his mouth dry, he comes face to face with his own greed. He realizes that he will likely not have enough time to get back to the starting point.

Though afraid of death, he could not stop. "After having run all that way they will call me a fool if I stop now," thought he. And he ran on and on, and drew near and heard the Bashkirs yelling and shouting to him, and their cries inflamed his heart still more . . .

Pahom looked at the sun, which had reached the earth: one side of it had already disappeared.

He took a long breath and ran up the hillock. It was still light there. He reached the top and saw the cap. Before it sat the Chief laughing and holding his sides. Pahom uttered a cry: his legs gave way beneath him, he fell forward and reached the cap with his hands.

"Ah, that's a fine fellow!" exclaimed the Chief. "He has gained much land!"

Pahom's servant came running up and tried to raise him, but he saw that blood was flowing from his mouth. Pahom was dead!

The Bashkirs clicked their tongues to show their pity.

His servant picked up the spade and dug a grave long enough for Pahom to lie in, and buried him in it. Six feet from his head to his heels was all he needed.

The Bashkir chief speaks just as Blankfein might, though the chief grasps better the moral absurdity of his seemingly generous offer to the peasant. In the interview, Blankfein said, "I don't want to put a cap on their ambition. It's hard for me to argue for a cap on their compensation." And yet, there is only so much time in a workday, a workweek, a lifetime. In the end, time is the one thing the greedy want more than anything. Tolstoy's story of the greedy peasant illustrates something that often gets left out in our descriptions of greed. Greed's excessive material acquisitiveness is built up over time and, in the end, is a distorted relation to our time on earth.

The death of Pahom was brought upon by a clash between two distinct ways of thinking about possessions and land. This conflict is present both within Pahom himself, indicated in the opening scene of the story, and later between Pahom and the Bashkirs. In the opening scene, Pahom notes that the peasant life is free of anxiety, but it is sustainable *over time*, resulting in a long and moderate life. But the opening scene also discloses Pahom's weakness for one possession in particular, "if only I had enough land." At the end of the story, the destructive potential of that internal conflict manifests in the difference between the Bashkir's worldview and Pahom's. For the Bashkirs, a human life is just as much measured by its temporality as its materiality. In a land of plenty, time imposes its own limitations. For Pahom, however, human desire knows no bounds other than the ambition of the heart and the wealth available from the land. Pahom lives as if *time didn't matter*, as if mortality and finitude were no match for human aspiration and a bountiful earth. Not until his final struggle to reach closure on his ambition, does the significance of the setting sun dawn on him.

The lesson of Tolstoy's story is that *time runs out* for each of us, and that when it does, we can't take our earthly treasures with us. We may be inclined to say, "Fair enough, time imposes limits on our ambitions. That's an old lesson." The point is more fundamental: the problem of time and mortality is precisely what motivates material greed in the first place. The fact that time runs out on all of us is not only an imposition placed externally on the desires of greed, but rather, fuels *excessive attachment to material goods precisely in a deluded effort to stop time.*

We like to say that greed hoards, but what is hoarding? Indeed, hoarding is a gathering of the world to the self, and thus intimately related to pride. But why hoard? Hoarding is an immoderate desire to possess. But why seek possession of anything for oneself at all? To possess is to take hold of something for oneself by *securing the presence of that which is otherwise ephemeral.* Possession gives a sense of permanence to the world. Attachment to things and places provides stability against the onslaught of time and change. Our possessions become totems of protection against death. This is why hoarding is accompanied by a pervasive anxiety over threats to one's possessions. The greedy person fears that what one possesses *now* will rot, rust, break, age, burn, depreciate, be stolen, deemed worthless, or in a word, die. The greedy person is the one who knows acutely that time moves on, that earthly goods fade away, that death awaits us all, and that our desires in this life cannot all be met. The greedy person knows all this, but in spite of it, they are driven to secure finite goods against the march of time toward death. These possessions protect us from the reality of impermanence that is the human condition.

The temporality of greed also explains why its desires impress such an urgency upon us. Greed proclaims, "I want *NOW!*" There is thus impatience inherent to greed. The greedy person not only wants new things, new possessions, and new attachments, it also seeks a perpetual confirmation that what one owns now is still present and will remain so. Hence the comfort that the greedy take in confirming their holdings, checking their stock numbers, monitoring the value of their house, or counting the books in their library, furnishings in their house, or friends on Facebook. The experience of possession itself is that it gives us a sense of the permanent. To own a home, versus to rent or to borrow money to own, is to tether one's individual strength and resilience to material goods. The problem with greed is thus twofold: it ascribes permanence to earthly things, and it gives the impression that an increase in possessions gives us some control over time. The question then is how can the human relation to time be re-imagined from vice to virtue?

Hope and the Redemption of Time

Christian hope offers a virtuous alternative to greed. At first glance, such a pairing would seem misplaced. Temperance might seem a more fitting virtue to quell avarice's ravenous desires. Simplicity, in as much as it is a virtue, may also be up to the task. Certainly, these are both good character traits to nurture. But in as much as greed entails a distorted relation to our finite temporality, hope offers a more radical corrective to avarice. A human life is one of movement and change. To be alive is to exist between birth and death, to create a past and desire a future, to endure hardship and be sustained over time. To be human is to exist in and through time. Hope, then, names the virtue through which we live well into the time we are given.

Narrative Time

In order to move from the temporality of greed to the temporality of hope, we must reflect more generally about time. In order for one to live virtuously with regard to time, time cannot be simply a series of years, weeks, days, or seconds. Such an abstract and scientific conception of time inter-prets it as an endless series of "now" points, wherein one present flows into the next without incident. In such a view, the past *was* real once, but is no longer (except as something fixed as fact in the present). The future is not real yet, since it is yet to happen. Only the present moment, which has no duration, is real. The human experience of time, however, is different. Time is *meaningful*, *variable*, and *dynamic*. The past, present, and future are all meaningful and bleed into one another. When one speaks of being "haunted by the past," the past lingers in the present and leaks into the future. The future itself shapes how we imagine and act in the present, in light of hopes, dreams, and desires not yet realized. Lived time, as opposed to clock time, is deeply rooted in our existential concerns and life projects.

The existential meaning of time shows up in the narrative character of life. Abstract ethical principles and maxims must be *lived out in the course of a life*, and the course of a life is structured as a narrative. In the recent revival of virtue ethics in both philosophical and theological discussions, there has been a parallel interest in the role of the *narrative imagination* in the moral life. Christian ethicists in particular have looked to narrative ethics because they have found the modern analytical approaches to moral philosophy wanting. Philosopher Charles Guignon articulates the connection between narrative and moral identity in his book *On Being Authentic*.

> What determines personal identity is . . . the continuous, ongo-ing, open-ended activity of living out a story *over the course of time*. . . . Just as we impart meaning to events by telling them to ourselves and to others, we are constantly imparting cohesive-ness and coherence to our lives by enacting a life story in our actions. Seen from this standpoint, we are not just tellers of a story, nor are we something told. We are a telling.[8]

If we ourselves are fundamentally a telling, artifacts like novels and movies are only possible because we are first and foremost narrative beings. Narra-tive is not only the work of poets, dramatists, and novelists reflecting upon chaotic life events that had no narrative order before one was imposed by the writer. "Stories are lived before they are told."[9]

Christian ethicist Stanley Hauerwas claims that in order to know our-selves, stories are necessary. Stories "are not replaceable by some other kind of account."[10] On an individual level, when a person lacks a sense of their own narrative, their life appears simply a sequence of unrelated events that

8. Guignon, *On Being Authentic*, 127.

9. MacIntyre, *After Virtue*, 211–12.

10. Hauerwas, *Hauerwas Reader*, 77.

renders joy, suffering, loss, birth and death unintelligible. To have a sense of self is to have a biography, a story to tell, and a plot to enact. Not only do we tell stories to make sense of our psyches and selves, we often think of moral decisions in terms of narratives. As Jim Cheney writes, "To contexualize ethical deliberation is, in some sense, to provide a narrative or story, from which the solution to the ethical dilemma emerges as a fitting conclusion."[11]

Hope and Uncertinaty

In telling or listening to a story, one must take measure of the now and the not-yet. Contemporary philosopher Alasdair MacIntyre points out that stories are not simply one thing happening after another, nor do they confirm things the listener already knows by other means. Stories possess two structural elements that set them apart from other modes and shape our engagement of them. The first element is that stories are *teleological*; that is, they move the listener from one place to somewhere else. The action and events have a trajectory, often expressed through the building of tension or complexity leading toward a resolution. As stories, and not say, doctrines or propositional truth claims, the stories must hide or delay the resolution. The narrative experience requires this hiddenness. Therefore, the second element of narratives is their *unpredictability*. Narratives are underdetermined. To hear a story told well is to be held in suspense because everything is not given nor easily anticipated in the present moment. At any given point, the listener does not know what will happen next. The art of good storytelling is navigating both their *teleology and unpredictability.*

These two elements are important to keep in mind when we make the connection between narrative and ethics. In our ethical decision making we often want certainty, clarity, and resoluteness. We want to know that the right conseqences will follow from the right actions or choices. A neat fit between right action and right consequence, however, is not usually possible in our world. We often have to settle for the unpredictability characteristic of complex situations with multiple human actors that complicate any easy transition from chosen action to predictable consequence. Ethical decision making is teleological, but also unpredictable. We live out our lives by imagining a possible shared future, that is, a future in which certain possibilities beckon us forward, others repel us and seem already foreclosed, and others perhaps inevitable. There is no present that is not informed by some image of some future and an image of the future that always presents itself in the form of a *telos*. MacIntyre writes, "Unpredictability and teleology therefore

11. Cheney, "Eco-Feminism and Deep Ecology," 144.

coexist as part of our lives; like characters in a fictional narrative we do not know what will happen next, but nonetheless our lives have a certain form which projects itself toward our future."[12]

As Christians, we become who we are, and embody the virtues we do, when we become actors in the story of salvation. In this context, hope is the virtue of living into the uncertainty and teleology of our lives well.

This tension between uncertainty and teleology is central to Luther's conception of hope. Luther is known, of course, for his treatments of faith as central to the Christian life, but hope is just as important in his theology. Indeed, in many of his writings hope functions as a synonym of faith. In his treatment of hope, Luther makes a distinction between the hopes of "people in general" and of "Christians." Both forms of hope entail a desire for the future realization of something not yet present. Both entail some degree of uncertainty, though the respective reasons for such uncertainty differ. Finally, both are founded on some reason for confidence (i.e., neither is absurd.)

For Luther, Christian hope requires a different attitude than reasonable expectation. Hope requires one be disposed toward God. Because of this, Christian hope is uncertain of the final goodness that God promises, but is certain that God is faithful to bringing forth that goodness. In relation to God's promise of reconciliation, hope entails a profound joy, reassurance, comfort, and delight. It provides affirmation of God's ongoing reconciliation with humanity and assurance through periods of doubt and anxiety. It is important to remember, nevertheless, that this disposition should not be equated with *self-confidence*. The archenemy of faith, in Luther's eyes, is egoism. The hope that gives strength and courage is not some form of "positive thinking" or psychological condition of confidence that one has generated through one's own efforts. Hope remains always a *response* to the word of promise that was given *by God* in the gospel.[13]

Hope, nevertheless, is as much constituted by certainty as it is uncertainty. The uncertainty inherent in hope becomes particularly acute in relation to one's personal salvation. At any given moment in this life, the religious individual does not overcome its alienation from, nor indeed opposition to God; salvation is never fully experienced as a present reality but is always experienced as delayed and yet to be achieved. Even upon receiving grace and being deemed righteous before God, Luther reminds us that

---

12. MacIntyre, *After Virtue*, 216.

13. Althaus expands on this warning of reducing hope into some kind of self-motivated courage to overcome the difficulties of religious life. Althaus, *Theology of Martin Luther*, 53.

a person remains simultaneously both righteous and sinful: *simmul iustus et peccator.*

The life of the religious individual is marked by what *is yet to come.* Luther emphasizes the antithesis for the sake of the synthesis, the negative for the sake of the positive. Particularly with regard to hope, Luther is overly careful not to turn hope's assurance into certain knowledge. Religious consciousness is never satisfied by its present completion; salvation is fully realized only in the future. The remoteness of God experienced through humiliation is never overcome in reality through hope to a comfortable, quietist faith. One may never presume to understand or possess God, but always must wait anxiously in hope and remain receptive to divine grace. In being marked by hope and not security or completion, the religious life exists simultaneously with religious doubt, anxiety, and trial while being driven by the hope that God will remain faithful to his promises. The remoteness of God is thus overcome *in hope,* as a present possibility of a future reality.

Nevertheless, like any of the virtues, hope effects change in the person. Hope changes the religious person into that which is hoped for, namely a person with whom God is reconciled. Hope itself is an essential component of the transformation of the person and one's turning toward the divine. Consider also Luther's commentary on Romans 15:13, "May the God of hope fill you."

> What a wonderful title, the "God of hope"! But this is the sign by which the apostle distinguishes between false gods and the True God. False gods are demons, gods of material things, because they possess those people who in their reliance on material things do not know how to hope. For he who relies on the true God, when all material things have been taken away, lives by pure hope alone. . . . Our joy and peace do not consist in something material, but are beyond material things, in hope. Otherwise the God of hope would not give them, for he gives good things which are hidden, joy in sadness and personal affliction, peace in the midst of tumult and outward persecution. Persecution causes hope to abound.[14]

Hope as the Corrective to Greed

In imagining the virtue of hope, we must see beyond a host of connotations associated with the word including wishful thinking, optimism,

---

14. Luther, *Lectures on Romans,* 414.

self-confidence. Hope engenders the proper posture toward time by orienting us toward God's word of *promise* that God is and will be faithful in the future. Hope not only anticipates the coming of the Lord in the eschaton, but adopts the pace of God's grace in our everyday lives now. That is to say, from the perspective of the virtue of hope, divine grace is not the gift of some good *thing*, but the gift of time.

Lest we think that the gift of time is merely the gift of *more* time, hope rather is a gift that redeems and reorients our being-in-time. Greed attempts to seize one's finite life back from the march of time and the inevitability of death. It attempts to defeat death both by buttressing one's self with the illusionary permanence of earthly possessions. Hope aligns one's desires with the pace of God's grace and movement within history; it becomes a sharing of the glory of God as it plays out in the story. This sharing acknowledges our finite, suffering, and mortal existence, by realizing that God's grace sustains us *over time*. Paul writes in Romans 5:1–5,

> Therefore, since we are justified by faith, we have peace with God through our Lord Jesus Christ, through whom we have obtained access to this grace in which we stand; and we boast in our hope of sharing the glory of God. And not only that, but we also boast in our sufferings, knowing that suffering produces endurance, and endurance produces character, and character produces hope, and hope does not disappoint us, because God's love has been poured into our hearts through the Holy Spirit that has been given to us.

As indicated in the Roman's passage, a virtue necessary to hope is forbearance. Peter Paris in his small book *Virtues and Values: The African and African American Experience* notes that forbearance has been a significant virtue for Africans and African Americans in particular because "each has had to endure a long-term dehumanizing plight of racial oppression, economic injustice, political disenfranchisement, and social ostracism. Under such bitter conditions, moral development was closely allied with the struggle for survival, and moral character was gradually formed in accordance with the virtue of forbearance."[15] There are strong parallels between this passage from Paris and the above passage from Paul.

The language I used above that hope realizes that God's "grace sustains us over time" sounds as if God calls us to a passive relationship to our own time. Hope, some would criticize, is the enemy of justice because it puts up for too long with too much hardship. Lest we think the waiting of

---

15. Paris, *Virtues and Values*, 30.

forbearance is merely passivity in the face of suffering, Paris continues by defending the wisdom inherent in effective forbearance.

> Doing what is necessary to preserve life under caustic condi-tions need not be viewed as either mindless submission or cow-ardice but, instead, as intelligent action. The collective wisdom of those who have lived for generations under such conditions may often be the most credible support for the spirit and prac-tice of forbearance. . . The virtue of forbearance also enabled both Afriacans and African Americans to give their assent to the philosophy of non-violent resistance long before it was named and articulated as such by Mahatma Gandhi. That is to say, it was not the philosophy of nonviolent resistance that inspired people's acceptance of it. Rather, it was generations of nonvio-lent practices that culminated in the virtue of forbearance and motivated people's acceptance of non-violence resistance as a philosophy.[16]

Forbearance is a necessary quality of character that must be cultivated on the way to genuine hope. Once hope takes root deep in the human per-son, its telos provides a future-oriented outlook for a life faithful to God. Hope allows one to look suffering in the face, resist it, and actively cooperate towards a future. Hope invigorates forbearance, gives it a purpose, and finds a hidden joy amidst the oppression of the present.

Consider, for example, Martin Luther's explanation of why we say "this day" and "daily" in the petition in the Lord's Prayer "Give us *this day* our *daily* bread." Luther cites two biblical passages, Proverbs 30:8–9 (a petition to be neither poor nor rich) and Matthew 6:34 (a command not to be anx-ious about tomorrow). He then comments, "These words teach us not to be greedy or wasteful or to worry about the future but to live contentedly in the confidence that the Lord will give us what we need."[17] Hope enables us to live futurally, stretched ecstatically into the promise that God will act in history. And yet, though hope is a sharing in God's glory, hope is not free of difficulty, suffering, or struggle. Only through suffering, endurance, and character formation over time can hope be realized within the human heart.

As joyously reassuring as it is to live in hope, however, we must remem-ber that Christian hope does not function like optimism, certainty, or even reasonable expectation. Hope does not calculate or weigh probabilities; it places us within the salvific narrative of God's grace as it unfolds over time. Philosopher Alasdair MacIntyre claims that, like a literary narrative, the

16. Ibid., 32.
17. Luther, *Large Catechism*, 98.

narrative form of human life has both *telos* and indeterminacy. We live into our stories, and as such, have a dual sense of both their orientation to future events and an ignorance of how these events will unfold. The problems with greed are many, but one of them is its frenzy to secure one's hoardings by a constant vigilance in order to eliminate all insecurity and doubt. Greed despises the delay of time, the uncertainty of the future, and the anxiety of our being-toward-death. In contrast, by relinquishing our own semblance of control of the future, hope trembles toward the hiddenness of God's grace and the fulfillment of his promise. Hope in the face of our mortality is not achieved through the denial of death or by stopping time, but by living in the now and the not yet through a reassuring and vulnerable reliance on God's grace.

Conclusion: Hope as the Anecdote to Greed

Hope offers a corrective to greed because both swing on the shared hinge of how we live in relation to time. Consider the description of the culture at Goldman Sachs, and the way it simultaneously provoked anxiety and greed. The mistake was, of course, that greed attempted to quell the anxiety over the inevitable passing of time by anchoring people to shifting moorings of material acquisition and possession.

The Christian life is not devoid of anxiety over mortality and loss. It is no trite thing to hand over our futures to God's history, which is promised but not yet actualized. Hope that does not tremble is not genuine hope. In this sense, hope does not eliminate difficulties or persecutions; but neither does it frantically cover them over with material acquisition and addictive attachments. Rather, hope *sustains us over time* through our present hardships toward a promised but hidden future. Abram's hope in that desolate land, as opposed to Lot's greed amidst luxury, did not end his difficulties immediately, but sustained him through them.

Greed is a *timely* vice in that it attempts to gather not only the world to ourselves and our immediate desires, but to take control of a future for these selfish ends. Hope is a *timely* virtue, because it recognizes that history is the Lord's, and that God's promise of salvation will satisfy the desires of the human heart, but only in the fullness of time.

5

ON BEING EMBODIED

Lust, Gluttony, and Temperance

If the body were easier to understand,
no one would have thought that we had a mind.[1]

—RICHARD RORTY

Aristotle, defender of the virtuous mean, understood temperance to moderate our appetites for sensual pleasures. He claimed that while ascetic insensitivity to pleasures was a vice rarely encountered, excessive attachment to pleasures was all too frequent among his fellow aristocrats. In his analysis, temperance made the twin appetites for food and sex virtuous, and thus he heralded in the Western moral imagination a now long-standing pairing of two distinct human desires. When we think about it, pairing a desire for food with a desire for sex might seem simplistic at best, and wrongheaded at worst. But as our literary history testifies, our imagination can't help but comingle these two desires. Temperance governs both, and thus counters the distortions of gluttony and lust. But how?

A simplistic grasp on the vices of gluttony and lust, however, can do more harm than good. Virtues are enabled by grace and directed toward love, but discerning temperance amidst gluttony and lust is fraught with risk. Secular and Christian culture alike reserve plenty of shame to heap

---

1. Rorty, cited in Pallassmaa, *Eyes of the Skin*, 17.

upon the gluttonous and the lustful. When misunderstood, a zeal for temperance only magnifies the culture of shame. We are just as likely to hear about the wages of the sin of gluttony, evidenced in the rising cases of obesity, cardiac disease, and diabetes, as we are of the sins of lust, evidenced in the increasing number of people addicted to Internet pornography, the public shaming of infidelity among politicians and celebrities, and international sex trafficking. As Simon Blackburn notes in his book *Lust*, "When something is both intensely desirable, and culturally identified as intensely shameful, we can expect psychic turmoil."[2] The cycle of shame and indulgence is common to the experience of both gluttony and lust. It is a cycle that temperance, properly understood, can correct. In this chapter, I hope to offer insight into how to think about these vices and virtues ethically. That is, I aim to provoke thought so that we might attend better to our own inner life of virtue and vice.

This is the only chapter that pairs two vices with a single virtue. Some explanation is in order. First, none of the pairings in this book are meant to be *the definitive* or *essential* pairings of the virtues corrective of a vice. Any number of virtues may assist one in turning one's soul away from vice and toward the Good. With regard to the sexual and culinary appetites, many virtues can steer human desires rightly: love can certainly be a corrective to lust, and justice can be a check upon gluttony. Each of the pairings of virtue and vice that I propose, however, does direct our attention to some key aspect of human life. When we examine temperance with regard to gluttony and lust, we bring to mind our embodiment and the vital energy that animates it. Human beings are essentially embodied in this life, and as the Apostles' Creed confesses, in the next as well. My hope is that by examining temperance, gluttony, and lust together, we will enable a more subtle view of these character traits.

Bodies and Their Vitality

The body and its desires are good. This is affirmed in the creation story, the incarnation of God in Christ, and the "resurrection of the body" affirmed in the Apostles' Creed. In the Judeo-Christian traditions, human *vitality* is the breath of life animating our embodied spirits. It finds particular expression in our desires for both food and sex. Consider how both of these basic desires ascribed to our human nature are named in the Genesis creation account.

2. Blackburn, *Lust*, 72.

"Be fruitful and multiply, and fill the earth and subdue it; and have dominion over the fish of the sea and over the birds of the air and over every living thing that moves upon the earth." God said, "See, I have given you every plant yielding seed that is upon the face of all the earth, and every tree with seed in its fruit; you shall have them for food. And to every beast of the earth, and to every bird of the air, and to everything that creeps on the earth, everything that has the breath of life, I have given every green plant for food." And it was so. God saw everything that he had made, and indeed, it was very good. (Gen 1:28–31)

Immediately following the creation event, God blesses our most basic needs as earthly bearers of God's image. Together, these mark the breath of life in each of us and our vitality to continue and produce life. Both desires are ordained good.

The body and these desires are part of our spiritual being, not set against it or a prison for it. While *vitality* speaks to the breath of life from the perspective of our bodies, it is integral to our whole being. Unfortunately, in our quest for intellectual, emotional, and spiritual maturity, the body often gets blamed for causing our spiritual failings. The apostle Paul's frequent contrasts between the life of the spirit and the life of the flesh would seem to give support for this dualistic idea. The life of the spirit and the life of flesh are both lived out, however, by the embodied spirits that we are. Our immediate experience of vital desires begs for a more nuanced description. C. S. Lewis reflects on the blame too frequently heaped upon the body.

> "You are always dragging me down," said I to my Body. "Dragging you down!" replied my Body. "Well I like that! Who taught me to like tobacco and alcohol? You, of course, with your idiotic adolescent idea of being 'grown-up.' My palate loathed both at first: but you would have your way. Who put an end to all those angry and revengeful thoughts last night? Me, of course, by insisting on going to sleep. Who does his best to keep you from talking too much and eating too much by giving you dry throats and headaches and indigestion? Eh?" "And what about sex?" said I. "Yes, what about it?" retorted the Body. "If you and your wretched imagination would leave me alone I'd give you no trouble. That's Soul all over; you give me orders and then blame me for carrying them out."[3]

Lewis' witty conversation between the body and soul attempts to overturn the oft-heard condemnation of the body. Whereas Plato held that harmony

---

3. Lewis, "Scraps," 216–17.

was achieved when the intellect controlled the rebellious and raucous bodily appetites, Lewis suggests that the intellect is always in control of the body. If the soul and its imagination are misguided or corrupted, the bodily appetites will follow suit. Lewis' description, however, still suggests a dualism between body and soul. The soul commands, and the body listens. In the immediate experience of virtuous or vicious sexuality and eating, however, the body and soul are not so separate. At times, when we experience a delightful dance, a celebratory meal, an impassioned embrace where one is attentive to the presence of the beloved—the body and spirit are more deeply unified. Frederich Beuchner phrases it with regard to sexuality, "Human beings are so hopelessly psychosomatic in composition that whatever happens to the soma [body] happens also to the psyche [soul] and vice versa."[4] The healthy person nurtured by a harmony between body and spirit is oriented toward the good as one unified being. As we shall see below, temperance brings this unity, simplicity, and contentment to the embodied spiritual beings that we are.

One of the ways a body/soul dualism plays our in our moral imagination is that we associate the body with animality and the soul with humanity. We compare the gluttonous and the lustful to beasts. But this is neither philosophically nor theologically fitting to what it means to live out our vitality in vicious or virtuous ways. Lest we equate vitality with mere physical instincts to consume calories and procreate, we must remember that we are talking about human beings who are made in the image of God. Human vitality—experienced so wonderfully in our embodied delights of eating a delicious meal amidst animated conversation, exercising strong and attuned muscles in a game of sport, dancing rhythmically and fluidly to music, or being aroused through the touch of our beloved—is not mere animal energy dressed up with cultural accouterments. Neither is it a physical state existing alongside a spiritual one. Philosophically speaking, human beings cannot be something other than human.[5] When we think of vices like gluttony or lust, it would be better to say that we are behaving as depraved humans, not animals. It's much less insulting to the animal kingdom.

As harmonious as our vitality can be, we must admit that it has a *wildness* inherent to it. But what do we mean by this term? Our vitality entails a dynamic open-ended desire, undisciplined in its inception, but malleable to our habituations. To be alive is to have this ecstatic excess of energy that pushes and pulls against the world. This quality of our vitality shows up in the excessive energy of children at play, the spontaneous desire for food

---

4. DeYoung, *Glittering Vices*, 166.

5. See Thomas Nagel's famous 1974 essay "What Is It Like to Be a Bat?"

we experience when hungry, and the impromptu dance of sexual arousal and intimacy. Wildness need not be a destructive chaos, but a playful and potentially creative sufeit that originates internal to the person.[6] Reflecting on the writings of Wendell Berry, J. Matthew Bonzo and Michael R Stevens describe what it would mean to honor the body's distinctive character.

> As the farmer cultivates the wild soil to bring forth life, so also we cultivate our bodies to become more human. The twin errors are present and possible again: one can leave the body an uncultivated wilderness, a chaos of immediate impulse and easy pleasures, unmoderated by any genuine discipline. Or one can overcompensate, overcultivate, to the point of hatred of the body, of strict constraints on bodily realities. Today's rejections of wilderness often involve a rejection of embodiment that is not so much ascetic as cosmetic. We have many more fitness centers, plastic surgeons, and Botox clinics in our suburbs than we do monasteries of flagellants on our street corners. The impulse to control is thus a manipulation that will play right up close to the sort of qualifications for the immoderate, appetitive life that we are loath to surrender: sex appeal is the result of our contemporary self-abnegation.[7]

The authors recognize the inherent wildness of our bodily appetites, but also the dual vices of not disciplining and over-controlling the wildness. Reminiscent of Aristotle, the authors seek a virtuous mean between the vicious extremes of insensibility and over-indulgence. Whereas Aristotle claims that vicious apathy toward pleasure is rarer than overindulgence, Bonzo and Stevens see a contemporary hatred of the body in our attempts to perfect it. A distorted view of the "ideal body," and the employment of technologies to bring it about, is destructive to a virtuous vitality. A proper love of one's embodied self does not define health as perfection, but as a cultivated wilderness.

When considering our bodies, we must also recognize our finitude and mortality. Despite a promise of immortality, our embodied vitality is limited. As individuals, we must to eat to live. We must receive physical touch to survive as infants, and flourish as adults. We are dependent upon others for all of these activities. The infant's relation to the mother after birth is fundamental to our human condition. None of us can walk with two legs shortly after birth; some of us can do this as children or adults; and very few of us can do it well shortly before death. The human body is not a static

6. See Gadamer, *Relevance of the Beautiful*, 23.
7. Bonzo and Stevens, *Cultivation of Life*, 104.

essence, and the virtues of it should not be either. We are rather a living and changing assemblage of capacities, all of which are finite, dependent on our environment's hospitality to these capacities, and communicative of our status to others. The "able-bodied" and "disabled" are both relative terms with respect to our assumptions of a normal environment (e.g., stairs versus ramps) and normal modes of dependency on others (e.g., canes versus someone else's arm). As I write these pages now, I await further news on my mother-in-law's condition, who has just suffered her third stroke in five years. The unity of mind and body, biology and spirituality, bears down on her and those caring for her. When considering her future, we become highly aware of the failures of built environments to accommodate her abilities. We see how her status as a person is immediately communicated to others through her changed ambulatory movements. We realize how vulnerable we must all be to one another if we are to meet each others' desires.

Our vitality is fragile, stretched precariously between birth and death, between our previous meal and our next, and between those who will be there for us in physical presence and those who will not. The virtues approach to ethics risks something in our moral imagination. With its emphasis on "excellence" and "human flourishing," we imagine such a life to be that of a fully mature, able bodied, and healthy adult. Historically speaking, the virtuous person was typically male and of the dominant racial profile. Temperance, perhaps better than any of the other virtues, attunes us to our humble state as finite and fragile creatures perpetually in need of grace.

Putting these characteristics of our embodiment together, let us name the vital desires common to eating and sexuality, to which me might apply the virtue of temperance. There are three key characteristics of vitality that temperance makes excellent. Vitality entails a desire 1) for continuing life through self-preservation (food) and reproduction (sex); 2) for experiencing pleasure, arousal, and delight; and 3) for enacting community with others.

While these desires are natural to our embodied spiritual existence, they are also the desires of *finite and mortal* human beings. In the face of our body's mortality, inevitable sickness, and being-toward-death, vitality animates our desires for nourishment and procreation. In the face of sensual experiences that are fleeting, at times difficult or painful, and inevitably dulled through age, vitality makes possible pleasure and delight. In the face of lonliness and separation from others, our vitality works toward communion through bodily activity of meal sharing and sexuality. Generally speaking, gluttony and lust are those habituated dispositions of character that *inhibit, harm, or otherwise bring ruin to embodied life, pleasure, and community.*

THE MORBIDITY OF GLUTTONY AND LUST

If our desires for food and sex are united around these common features, these same desires can be distorted to bring ruin to that vitality. In this chapter we will weave between descriptions of gluttony and lust, not because they are the same vice, but because together they reveal the character of temperance as a virtue. Certainly lust and gluttony are distinct vices, as the practices of eating and sex are distinct. Their difference, however, rests in the difference between the initial desires that they distort. Once distorted, these vices resemble each other more than their original desires do.

Gluttony is a deadly sin perhaps more literally than any other. Each of the seven vices wreaks its own destruction on the person, but only gluttony so directly affects life's longevity. This truncated vitality affects both individuals, whose bodily health deteriorates through a vicious relationship to food, and societies, who starve and destroy their environments through overconsumption.

In the immediate experience, the glutton is incapable of making a meal anything more than an occasion for satisfying their insatiable need for consumption. Not all gluttonous consumption, however, is rooted in sheer excess. Gluttony takes many forms. Borrowing from a medieval formulation, contemporary Christian ethicist Rebecca Konyndyk DeYoung uses the acronym F.R.E.S.H. to articulate gluttony's varieties. Gluttony is the result of habitually "eating fastidiously, ravenously, excessively, sumptuously, hastily."[8] To be fastidious is to be so concerned with one's particular culinary pleasure that one consistently demands perfection in satisfying one's very particular desires. When ravenous, the glutton's singular pursuit of frenzied consumption dulls them to the pleasures and community that a meal makes possible. The hasty ensure their own plate is full before attending to others who still need food. The sumptuous are so enraptured by the pleasures of eating that they ignore the friendships, justice, and other goods that come from eating together. The excessive simply eat beyond fullness. Each of these forms of gluttony get in the way of the three goods central to virtuous eating: continuance of life, bodily pleasure, and community.

Gluttony not only interferes with sustaining of life, it limits the simple delights of eating. Our vitality makes possible the pleasure of eating, in the face of sensual experiences that themselves are fleeting, at times painful, and perhaps dulled through age or sickness. These delights are both physical and spiritual in character. Aristotle claims that temperance is an excellence of enjoying the pleasures of touch by achieving a mean between

8. DeYoung, *Glittering Vices*, 141.

excess indulgence and excess insensitivity. The mean is not some abstract proportion of consumption, but that which frees us to be present to our enjoyment. Comte-Sponville writes, "Temperance is that moderation which allows us to be masters of our pleasure instead of becoming its slaves. It is free enjoyment and hence better enjoyment, for it enjoys its own freedom as well."[9] A meal can be a wonderful source of bodily and spiritual pleasure, when its participants are free from both starvations and addictions. In the Christian moral imagination, we use the word grace to name that aspect of the delights of life made possible when we are freed from sin and broken-ness. In the Christian moral imagination, we use the word *grace* to name that aspect of the delights of life made possible when we are freed from sin and brokenness. The pleasures that temperance makes possible are graced enjoyment and hence better enjoyment, for they enjoys its own grace. The glutton chains himself to food so strongly that the delights of graced enjoyment are lost.

When it comes to lust, we must remember that lust is not to be equated with strong sexual desire. Lust is, in our context, a vice and thus a distortion of an otherwise good human desire. With tabloid headlines aplenty to serve up illustrations, let us rather turn to two classical descriptions of lust. In 371 CE a young, pre-conversion St. Augustine arrived at the university in Carthage. In his masterpiece, *Confessions*, he recounts the state of his soul upon entering the city.

> I came to Carthage and all around hissed a cauldron of illicit loves. As yet I had never been in love and I longed to love; and from a subconscious poverty of mind I hated the thought of being less inwardly destitute. I was in love with love, and I hated safety and a path free from snares. My hunger was internal, deprived of inward food, that is of you yourself, my God. But that was not the kind of hunger I felt. I was without any desire for incorruptible nourishment, not because I was replete with it, but the emptier I was, the more unappetizing such food became. So my soul was in rotten health. . . . I rushed headlong into love, by which I was longing to be captured. "My God, my mercy," in your goodness you mixed in much vinegar with that sweetness. My love was returned and in secret I attained the joy that enchains. I was glad to be in bondage, tied with the troublesome chains, with the result that I was flogged with the red hot iron rods of jealousy, suspicion, fear, anger, and contention. . . . I polluted the spring waters of friendship with the filth of concupiscence.[10]

9. Comte-Sponville, *Small Treatise on the Great Virtues*, 39.

10. Augustine, *Confessions*, 35.

In Christian theological circles, it is almost cliché to reference Augustine in theologies of sexuality. Augustine's own theological and autobiographical analyses of desire, emotion, and sexuality are both brilliant and idiosyncratic. But what actually is lustful in Augustine's account above? Looking at his experience, we note several characteristics. First, we note something that occurs over and over again in Western theological and literary traditions: Augustine describes lust through the metaphors appropriate to gluttony. In Augustine's account we read "a cauldron of illicit loves," "my hunger was internal," "I was deprived of inward food." "desire of incorruptible nourishment," "unappetizing food," and "your goodness mixed vinegar and sweetness." Lust *consumes* what it desires. Second, we note another set of repeated metaphors appropriate to imprisonment: "captured," "bondage," and "chains." Lust *enslaves* the person. Finally, Augustine sets up a series of contrasts indicating a dichotomous experience: vinegar–sweetness, hunger–satiety, longing for love–ignorance of love, purity–filth. Lust *divides* the person. From such a description, we get an initial phenomenology of lust: the lustful are both divided and enslaved by their own excessive appetites for a pleasure that cannot be satisfied.

Now let us turn to another description of lust, this time in Shakespeare's Sonnet 129.

> The expense of spirit in a waste of shame
> Is lust in action: and till action, lust
> Is perjured, murderous, bloody, full of blame
> Savage, extreme, rude, cruel, not to trust,
> Enjoy'd no sooner but despised straight,
> Past reason hunted, and no sooner had
> Past reason hated, as a swallow'd bait
> On purpose laid to make the taker mad;
> Mad in pursuit and in possession so;
> Had, having, and in question to have, extreme
> A bliss in proof, and proved, a very woe;
> Before, a joy proposed; behind, a dream.
> All this the world well knows; yet none knows well
> To shun the heaven that leads men to this hell.

The main contrast Shakespeare's sonnet is structured according to is temporal: before and after. The lustful anticipate that satisfying their desires will bring joys, bliss, even heaven itself. After acting out their lust, however, they are tormented by shame, woe, and a journey back to hell. His opening and closing speak to the pattern of shame and indulgence that marks the compulsive desires of gluttony and lust alike. The second repeated theme in this Sonnet is lust's distortion of reality. Like many addictions, the temporary ignorance that besets the lustful distorts their perception and reason. Lust looks beyond reason, leads to madness, tells lies to itself, and trades on a willed ignorance.

For both Augustine's and Shakespeare's accounts, lust wreaks havoc in the soul. That said, neither account speaks to its enactment upon others, which often does more damage. Any number of thinkers, from Aristotle to Lewis to DeYoung, blame lust's insensitivity to others on its excessive desire for pleasure. As C. S. Lewis describes in his book on the *Four Loves*, "We use a most unfortunate idiom when we say, of a lustful man prowling the streets, that he 'wants a woman.' Strictly speaking, a woman is just what he does not want. He want's a pleasure for which a woman happens to be the necessary piece of apparatus."[11] Behind Lewis's description is another critique of lust: Lust *objectifies* the other person by making one's own pleasure the highest good. If indeed that was the case, then lust would seem *tout court* to be vicious. Insightful as Lewis' pithy description is, it is not quite accurate. Lust may just as easily be motivated by a desire for power, relief from grief, or compulsion from addiction. The point being that lust is not problematic so much because of its excessive elevation of pleasure, but because of its dismissal of or harm to the vitality of the other person.

Philosopher Martha Nussbaum, in an important article titled "Objectification," outlines seven different ways that objectification can happen through vicious sexual desire and practices. Each is lustful in its own distinct way, because each limits the full participation of both parties in sexual desire or practices.

1. *Instrumentality*: The objectifier treats the object as a tool of his or her purposes.

2. *Denial of autonomy*: The objectifier treats the object as lacking in autonomy and self-determination.

3. *Inertness*: The objectifier treats the object as lacking in agency, and perhaps also in activity.

4. *Fungibility*: The objectifier treats the object as interchangeable (*a*) with other objects of the same type, and/or (*b*) with objects of other types.

5. *Violability*: The objectifier treats the object as lacking in boundary-integrity, as something that it is permissible to break up, smash, break into.

---

11. Lewis, *Four Loves*, 94.

6. *Ownership*: The objectifier treats the object as something that is owned by another, can be bought or sold, etc.

7. *Denial of subjectivity*: The objectifier treats the object as something whose experience and feelings (if any) need not be taken into accout.[12]

When any of these become habituated dispositions to act towards others, the person inflicts their lust on the other. These are not merely deprivations of our character, but do outright harm to others and the community.

In the end, gluttony and lust are those habituated dispositions of character that *inhibit, harm, or otherwise bring ruin to embodied life, pleasure, and community*. Together, these three goods are characteristic of our vitality, and each of them is denatured by our vicious habits. The question then becomes, what does virtuous vitality look like? Temperance offers an excellence fitting to our embodied souls.

TEMPERANCE AND THE WHOLE OF THE VIRTUOUS LIFE

Many in today's culture, and especially Christians, associate temperance with abstinence. As I check the dictionary on my laptop, for example, the first definition for *temperance* reads "abstinence from alcoholic drink." In our own history, temperance evokes memories of the "Temperance Movement," which was really an abstinence movement, which itself led to prohibition. Temperance is thus typically seen negatively, for we assume it means to limit, stifle, deny, or suppress something altogether. Just say No!" might be the mantra of such a view of temperance—no to food, no to sex, no to pleasure all together. While many of these connotations have been part of our recent associations, such meanings distort a richer interpretation offered through the longer history of the virtue.

An ancient definition of temperance still holds sway: *temperance is moderation in sensual desires*. The question is, of course, what does moderation entail and from where does it receive its guidance. In its original Greek context, temperance (*sophrosyne)* was a difficult concept to explain or teach. Though any virtue is situated within a given culture's mores, and thus only fully understandable in that context, *sophrosyne* is a subtle virtue that is rarely articulated outright. There was no clear exemplar of temperance, the way a soldier was for courage, the politician for justice, or the philosopher for wisdom. *Sophrosyne* is characteristic of the Greek *ethos*, or *way of being*, more than any explicit set of moral rules or guidelines. *Sophrosyne* was tied

12. Nussbaum, "Objectification," 57.

up with what it meant to be a good Greek, and to lack the quality would be cause for shame. In this sense, the temperate has a cultivated *attentiveness* to what was expected of one.[13] Though *sophrosyne* is often translated moderation, it is difficult to find an outright English equivalent. Swedish culture, actually, has a closer term—*lagom*—that operates with much of the spirit of Greek *sophrosyne*. In Swedish culture *lagom* means something like "just the right amount," "moderation," or "appropriate." *Lagom* is actually a shorting of an older Viking term "laget om" which literally translated is "around the team," indicating it as a communal sensibility. The term is understood intuitively only by living within the culture for some time.

In its most ancient context, temperance operated as a humbling virtue, keeping those with wealth and power grounded amidst their tendency to excess, aggrandizement, and *pleonexia* (excessive and unruly desires). As a corrective, temperance was also associated with the command to "Know thyself!" The iconic Greek command to self-knowledge was inscribed above the entrance to the holy site of Greek Wisdom, the Temple at Delphi. Werner Jaeger, in his exceptional study of Greek culture *Paideia: The Ideals of Greek Culture*, explains this connection:

> At Delphi the educational power of Greek religion reached its maximum, and spread from there far beyond the frontiers of Hellas. The wise sayings of sages were dedicated to Apollo and inscribed in his temple, since their worldly wisdom was only a reflection of divine wisdom. "*Know thyself*"—the doctrine of *sophrosyne*, by which men learn to remember the limits of human power and ambition. . . . The moderation that Apollo preached was not the humdrum doctrine of peace and contentment. It was a strong repression of the new individualistic impulse to wantonness; for in the Apolline code, the worst of the outrages against heaven was "not to think human thoughts"—to aspire too high, beyond the limits fixed for man.[14]

In both the ancient Greek and later Medieval Christian traditions, temperance is the humblest cardinal virtue. As Christian theology takes up the virtue tradition, temperance often commands less respect than other holy virtues, perhaps because it is a virtue of the "lower" parts of the soul—the body and its appetites. Wisdom, in contrast, is an intellectual virtue. Justice and courage lead one to great actions or societies. Thomas Aquinas notes in his *Summa Theologica* that courage and justice are more admirable and wisdom is more necessary than temperance. That said, he also noted

13

14. Jaeger, *Paideia*, 167.

that temperance is the most difficult virtue to attain. Twentieth-century Christian thinker Josef Pieper argues that temperance is of less importance because "discipline and moderation and chastity are not [themselves] the fulfillment of man," which presumably would entail the excellences of higher capacities.[15] André Comte-Sponville sums up the humility of temperance well when he says, "[Temperance] is not a virtue meant for extraordinary circumstances, but an ordinary, humble virtue, to be practiced on a regular basis, a virtue of moderation, not heroism."[16] In our own society, replete with natural and economic resources, temperance also does not carry the admiration it should. Most political communities don't give out medals for the most temperate citizen, nor do we send biographies of consistently self-controlled individuals up the best-seller charts.

But why shouldn't we? Communities of recovering addicts rightfully give temperance the honor it is due. Why don't the rest of us? I would imagine that we likely downplay the virtue of moderation in our society because temperance seems at best a rather mundane character trait not as obvious an *excellence* as other virtues. Occasionally we do celebrate temperance, but typically only for those whose lives have crashed and burned and who have since gotten their lives back under control, whereas the "rest of us" don't need such help. As most of us know, however, the tendencies, risks, and temptations of gluttony and lust are only too real. In a world of excess, adopting moderation would do us well. Perhaps the most significant place in which temperance gets its rightful due is among environmentalists and those concerned with global hunger and extreme poverty. Temperance, indeed, may be the only virtue to save our societies from collapsing under their own excess.

Temperance as Simplicity

In many situations, we associate temperance with the desire for simplicity. If, as Dante says, lust, gluttony, and greed each entail *excessive desires for secondary things*, then tempering these excesses might be possible by embracing a simpler way of life. Before Dante, the Stoic philosophers thought simplicity of desires brought peace to the soul—this in contrast to the turmoil brought on by a neediness for decadent pleasures. In our own day, consider the mantra of our resistance to consumerism or the rat race of middle-class America: "Simplify your life!" In this regard, temperance corrects the *excessiveness* of lust and gluttony similarly to how it would correct

15. Pieper, *Virtues of the Human Heart*, 33.
16. Comte-Sponville, *Small Treatise on the Great Virtues*, 42.

greed. But temperance as simplicity does something more basic than put-ting a cap on pleasure. Temperance brings simplicity to the whole of the virtuous soul. The tradition behind this interpretation begins with Plato.

Plato's treatment of temperance highlights a specific characteristic of the virtue. Plato notes, in the *Republic*, that *temperance is a virtue for the soul as a whole.* To the extent that a human soul can be said to have differ-ent "parts" with corresponding desires—the intellectual and its desire for wisdom, the spirited and its desire for honor and ambition, and the bodily and its sensual appetites—temperance is the virtue of harmony and right order among the parts. Temperance harmonizes the whole of the soul so that the intellect's desire for wisdom may lead the soul's other desires toward goodness. In other words, the virtue of wisdom is powerless without the virtue of temperance. To bring disparate parts into a harmonious whole is to simplify that which is complicated. To appreciate simplicity as a form of temperance, we might consider simplicity theologically as a characteristic of God. Though we will not examine the idea in depth, a brief introduction to the concept of divine simplicity will help orient us to our chief concern, simplicity as a form of temperance.

According to the classical theism of the middle ages, from Augustine to Anselm to Aquinas, *God is radically simple.* Some form of the doctrine of divine simplicity is present in Jewish and Islamic thought as well. In this regard, God is unlike any creature, each of which posses complexity and composition. God is not *composed* of parts, material, spatial, or even tem-poral. God simply is. In contrast, we as human beings can be said to be made up of different types of matter, perhaps also a psyche, or maybe even a soul, that combine together to make us and could combine together to make something else. We might also express our identity temporally in terms of stages of growth—I am who I am *because* of my infancy, my childhood, my early adulthood, etc. God is not like this. The Creator cannot be composed of the creation. In the language of philosophy, the doctrine of divine sim-plicity holds that there is no real distinction between God as the subject of God's attributes, on the one hand, and God's attributes, on the other. God is not God *and also* just. God is just. God is not God *and also* wise. God is wise. God is what God is. God is identical to God's nature. St. Augustine states it thus:

> We speak of God in many ways—as great, good, wise, blessed, true, and whatever else does not seem unworthily said of him. Nonetheless, God is identical with his greatness, which is his wisdom (since he is not great by virtue of quantity, but by virtue of power); and he is identical with his goodness, which is his

wisdom and his greatness; and he is identical with his truth, which is all of these things. For in him it is not one thing to be blessed and another to be great, or wise, or true, or to be good, or to be altogether himself.[17]

Anselm in his *Proslogion* declares, "Life, wisdom, and all the rest are not parts of you [God], but all are one, and each of them is the whole of what you are and the whole of what the others are."[18] And Aquinas puts it this way in his *Summa Contra Gentiles*: "In every simple thing, its being and that which it is are the same. For if the one were not the other, simplicity would be removed. As we have shown, however, God is absolutely simple. Hence, in God, being good is not anything distinct from him; he is his goodness."[19] William Valicella, writing in the *Stanford Encyclopedia of Philosophy*, puts it this way: "God is not only radically non-anthropomorphic, but radically non-creaturomorphic, not only in respect of the properties he possesses, but in his manner of possessing them. God, we could say, differs in his very ontology from any and all created beings."[20]

It is helpful if we consider why we are not simple the way God is simple. We have a multitude of desires, conflicts of emotions, and contradictory beliefs. We convert and leave behind old ways, we aspire to be something we are not yet, and we doubt whether we will be up for the task. We can lose our bodily heath simultaneous with gaining spiritual well-being. We can perfect our physical strength and lack emotional fortitude.

Though we cannot achieve divine simplicity, we can reimagine what it could mean for the person. Consider simplicity as an attribute of a person. Bring before your mind a virtuously simple person. Resist the pejorative equations of simplicity with simplemindedness or a simple soul with a st-impleton. Rather, imagine a person who enjoys the goodness of simplicity and in whom simplicity is a praiseworthy mark of their character. In this regard, the simple person is straightforward, not duplicitous; plainspoken, not grandiose; aware, not self-conscious. They are without pretensions, ulterior motives, or guile. Comte-Sponville describes such a person poetically:

> Simplicity is nakedness, dispossession, poverty, its only wealth everything, its sole treasure nothingness. Simplicity is freedom, lightness, transparency. Simple as air, free as air: simplicity is

---

17. Augustine, *De Trinitate*, 6.7.8

18. Anselm, *Proslogion*, 18.

19. Aquinas, *Summa Contra Gentiles*, I 38.

20. Valicella, "Divine Simplicity," para. 1.

airiness of thought, a window open to the grand breath of the
world, to the infinite and silent presence of all things.[21]

The simple person breathes contentedly with their ordinariness, and
yet such people are far from common. They are silent, attentive, and above
all present to that which is before them. They live without pride, without
remorse, without the burdens of doubt or proclamations of certainty. The
simple person exists truly as an individual—not set apart over and above
others, or overtly separated from the crowd—but as a singular dignity of
human presence, open to the gift and wonder and suffering of others. This
is the ideal that Plato alludes to when he sees temperance as a virtue of the
soul as a whole that brings harmony to discordant desires.

RESTORING VITALITY THROUGH TEMPERANCE

Shannon Jung writes extensively about Christian practices surrounding
food and eating. In many of his texts, Jung celebrates the joy and delight
made possible by food. The word he uses to describe such joy is *jouissance*.
He writes, in his book *Sharing Food: Christian Practices of Enjoyment*,

> *Jouissance* is much more profound than just good feelings or
> even mindful eating, though it incorporates those. Jouissance is
> a matter of deep joy, of assured security, of living in the presence
> of God, as though the kingdom had come indeed. So this is not
> just a matter of enjoying our food, but a claim that *we can be
> transformed*. The eating practices the church has discovered and
> established over the generations are part and parcel of the path
> that will lead us to abundant life, to *abbondanza*.[22]

Pleasure is a good. Its existence in our lives affirms the goodness of
our bodies, senses, emotions, and memories. To experience hunger without
malnourishment is to anticipate something good. The anticipation of a feast
is an involuntary and hopeful wonder at what is to come. Jung notes that the
involuntary reactions of our bodies to the thought and anticipation of food
is a wonder to behold. "Food is so much more engaging than it would need
to be if it were only about sustaining life. God made food appetizing—not
only nutritious."[23] Unfortunately, gluttony mutes the deep pleasures of being alive to our senses and desires that good food practices make possible.

21. Comte-Sponville, *Small Treatise on the Great Virtues*, 151.

22. Jung, *Sharing Food*, 145.

23. Ibid., 25.

Gluttony robs us of the pleasures of anticipation, the pleasures of consumption, and the pleasures of satiation.

Before the meal begins, the temperate can sit without anxiety and await the feast. They know well the joy of taking time to enact the rituals in the *preparation of* food with one's family or friends, the mild delight in slight nibbling and tasting that whets the appetite without voracity, and the wonder at the artistry, simple or complex, that patient and skilled preparation evokes. The glutton has no such patience, fixated as they are on the always too delayed consumption itself. When the meal proper does ensue, the glutton prevents the kind of *joussiance* that Jung claims marks joyous gratitude for the pleasures of the meal. With regard to the pleasures of eating well, Jung notes how gluttony shows up in the overabundance of food in our society, in the instant availability of its consumption, and in the solitary practices of eating cheap food that many in our society adopt. "Junk food, quickly prepared, thoughtlessly eaten, eaten alone or in front of the TV, and scarfed down—how can these practices not impact us? Is this abundant life? The ready accessibility and relative low cost of food leads to unappreciative eating, obesity, and poor health. It can also lead to attenuated relationships and to the transmission of misperceptions to our children. Rather than contributing to the delight and the enjoyment of our households, these dynamics have reduced the joy and quality of our lives."[24] Finally, at the conclusion of the meal, gluttony again prevents the contentment of satiation. As Comte-Sponville notes, "How sad, [the gluttons] say, to be not in the least bit hungry or thirsty. Its because they want more, always more, and don't even know how to be content with excess. That's why the debauched are sad, that's why alcoholics are unhappy. Indeed, what could be more depressing than a glutton who has had his fill?"[25]

Again we return to the theme of simplicity: the simple pleasures of patient food preparation with good ingredients, the simple pleasures of savoring eating amidst hunger, and the simple pleasures of being content with the enacted ritual of eating in community. Bruce Marshall notes that "Jesus had the temerity to suggest that the table-fellowship shared with disciples, tax collectors, and sinners constituted an anticipation of the kingdom of God. He proclaimed the presence of the kingdom in the eating and drinking and laughing of those occasions."[26]

The pleasures of satiety and the freedom from neediness are all impossible for the truly lustful and gluttonous. While the intemperate scorn

24. Ibid., 145.
25. Comte-Sponville, *Small Treatise on the Great Virtues*, 41.
26. Jung, *Sharing Food*, 17.

any limitations on their desires imposed by outdated cultural or religious conventions, they become prisoners of their own neediness and internal discord. The temperate, on the other hand, are not incapable of enjoying the occasional delights that come from either an exquisitely prepared meal or a particularly passionate sexual embrace. The temperate person does not make decadence the standard for enjoyment, but finds contentment in ordinary vitality perhaps best modeled in the simplicity of the Eucharist itself, where bread and wine can make for a holy feast.

Temperance and Sexuality

Lust prevents us from realizing the goods of sexual desire and practice. Sexual desire affirms three fundamental goods of human embodiment: the goodness of reproduction, pleasure, and intimacy. These three correspond to vitality shared by eating and sexuality: continuance of life, pleasure, and community. Temperance is the virtue that promotes the realization of these goods through the cultivation of individual and communal excellences. While it is commonplace to say that lust's chief distortion is that it places pleasure above all else, the distortions of lust are as complex as the excellences of good sexuality.

In the face of our body's mortality, inevitable sickness or decline, and being-toward-death, vitality animates our desires for procreation. God ordains the regeneration of new life. Regardless of whether any one of us has children of our own, each of us is a participant in the continuation of life simply from the fact that we are the result of the sexual union of others. Not all are called or desire to have children. And yet we are each called to participate in the regeneration of life. This can occur through a variety of practices: growing food, feeding others, being hospitable to others in our homes, having families and children of our own, adopting the children of others, or caring for those in their journey between birth and death. When virtuous, our sexuality is integrated into the larger good of the continuation of life among the people of God. Good sex practices, and the desires that make them possible, honor the wonder and power of reproduction. This is the case whether the couple desire in the moment to have a child or not, or whether the couple is biologically capable of having a child or not. Sexual coupling affirms the dignity of life, self-preservation, and ongoing generations of family.

In the face of sensual experiences that are themselves fleeting, at times painful, and perhaps dulled through age or sickness, our vitality makes possible pleasure and delight. Aristotle claims that temperance is an excellence of enjoying the pleasures of touch when it achieves a mean between excess indulgence and excess insensitivity. Comte-Sponville writes, "Temperance is that moderation which allows us to be masters of our pleasure instead of becoming its slaves. It is free enjoyment and hence better enjoyment, for it enjoys its own freedom as well."[27] A meal can be a wonderful source of bodily and spiritual pleasure when its participants are free from starvation and from addictions. The pleasures of sexual intimacy are enhanced when freed from the frenzy of neediness or exertion of power. In the Christian moral imagination, we use the word grace to name that aspect of the delights of life made possible when we are freed from sin and brokenness. The pleasures that temperance makes possible are graced enjoyment and hence better enjoyment.

In our sexual practices, graced enjoyment is the pleasure of mutual self-giving, bodily touch, and the wonder of desire. The lustful are incapable of such pleasures, precisely because they are incapable of being content with pleasure. When lust resembles a gluttony for sexual pleasure, it fails to trust pleasure—it panics in the face of its fleeting nature or it greedily demands it be of a certain quality or variety. On the other hand, the goods of sexual pleasure are only enhanced by temperance, for temperance allows for the transformation of the commonplace, the enlivening of the ordinary. It does not demand that the orgasmic ecstasies that sometimes accompany sexual union became the standards of intimacy. It does not seek to control the moment or the performance so as to get a handle on pleasure. Rather it seeks to be receptive to the other. Julie Hanlon Rubio, in her book *Family Ethics: Practices for Christians*, asks the following: "Can sex be understood as a practice like prayer, fasting, or simplicity? . . . [Can it be an] intentional, shared action, situated in the context of a tradition, ordinary in outward appearance but transcendent in its association with fundamental human goods."[28]

What is the simplicity of our sexuality? In a primary sense, through sex a couple seeks connection amidst duality. They seek honesty amidst duplicity. They seek to be themselves to each other, and to break free from the tangled web of role playing and psychological projections. Good sex involves both partners present as themselves for the other, able to tolerate the anxiety that such vulnerability and intimacy may entail. Nakedness itself signifies the vulnerability of being *simply* ourselves, as ourselves, before the other and they before us. Temperance thus encourages a disposition toward presence, transparency, and freedom. It is to touch and be touched

---

27. Comte-Sponville, *Small Treatise on the Great Virtues*, 39.
28. Rubio, *Family Ethics*, 99.

in the presence of each other's singular dignity, in light of the ordinariness of our imperfect bodies and souls. Simplicity does not demand perfection, nor hold before oneself or one's partner an ideal of purity as such. The temperate person can be their very ordinary and finite self, capable of being present and transparent to the world and others. This is precisely what is lost with lust; simplicity is replaced with complication, chaos, and cacophony. In place of being attentive, one seeks consumption; in place of being content, one suffers or enacts judgment; in place of being present, one anxiously avoids intimacy.

In the shared practices of sexuality, temperance pans out in terms of faithfulness. Faithfulness is the fitting response to the nature of sexuality—its simplicity, its vulnerability, its giftedness. Rubio says, "Vulnerability requires a disciplining of desires to a relationship, a reasonable limitation to free one's attention for one particular other. We say, in effect, 'I'm not going to any place or to anyone else. I'll pour my relational energy into you.'"[29] This is the heart of the goods of sexual pleasure and intimacy enabled through mutual trust, vulnerability, and generosity. Temperance enables moderation and simplicity of desire to increase pleasure, foster intimacy, and rejuvenate life. As Augustine says in *Of the Morals of the Catholic Church*, "Temperance is love giving itself completely to that which is loved."[30]

CONCLUSION

Temperance manifests the goodness, freedom, and pleasure human embodiment offers, by recognizing that the simplicity of one's vitality itself can be a sufficient measure for satisfying our desires. We live through the bodies we have, and these bodies are of different ages, ability, health, and history. Temperance enables contentment in the present stage of life we all find ourselves in, and guides how we enjoy that life with others through the practices of eating and sexuality.

The excesses of gluttony and lust disrupt the simple joys of our vitality by habituating it to fixate on something more than the present grants, something different than the ordinary offers, something beyond what existence promises. The pleasures of contentment and the freedom from neediness are impossible for the truly lustful and gluttonous. While the intemperate may scorn limitations on their desires that look like some outdated cultural or religious conventions, they themselves easily become prisoners of their own compulsions and internal discord. While in the throws of each, one

29. Ibid., 118.
30. Augustine, *Of the Morals of the Catholic Church*.

fails to live in the present because one obsesses over that which one does not have. These vices divide the person against himself or herself, disjoints them from the present, and diverts them into empty alleviations of their anxiety. With regard to lust, such internal chaos often does direct harm to others. Temperance is the virtue that restores health, balance, and simplicity to our most basic desires. Is such temperance easy to achieve? Certainly not! As Aquinas notes, while temperance is the most humble of the virtues, it is also the most difficult to maintain.

6

On Being Sanctified

Envy and Courage

> There is a thought that has haunted me for a long time.... It is to portray a
> wholly good person. Nothing is more difficult, especially in our time.[1]
>
> —Fyodor Dostoyevsky

COURAGE STANDS TALL AS the most universally recognized virtue across cultures. Indeed, it would be difficult to imagine a culture that would not praise a person who possesses the moral character to face adversity with resolve, suffering with endurance, and threats with an unwavering commitment to some good. That being said, courage is so universally admired that it seems in danger of being morally indiscriminate. Courage, it would seem, can serve both good and evil ends. Are thieves courageous when they overcome their fear and hold up a convenience store? Were the German SS soldiers courageous when they didn't let their fear of death interfere with advancing the Nazi front? Perhaps courage is morally neutral like strength or intelligence? Perhaps it gives people the fortitude to do what they desire, regardless of the goodness of the end. In no other virtue

1. "Letter to Maikov," 31 December 1867, as quoted in Edith Wyschogrod, *Saints and Postmodernism.*

do we face more strongly the critique of virtue ethics in general: virtues, unlike rules or right actions, are vague and hence too culturally relative to be helpful in making sound moral decisions.

Envy lay at the opposite end of the spectrum from courage. Envy would seem to be one of the most universally despised vices among the seven deadly sins. As we have seen, cultures sometimes recast vices into something praiseworthy: Ancient Greece found a virtue in pride, contemporary Western pop culture interprets lust as youthful vitality, and other cultures have seen gluttony as a sign of high social status. But envy, the insidious desire to take for one's own the goods enjoyed by another and the accompanying malice toward the envied, cannot be reinterpreted as a virtue. As Karl Olson wrote in his book on the seven virtues and vices, "Next to pride, envy is traditionally considered the 'worst' sin not because it is less loathsome than pride, which it is not, but because unlike pride, envy does not pretend to be godlikeness. It is, in fact, an admission of its opposite."[2]

That said, envy is a highly complex psychological phenomenon, capable of displaying great subtleties and disguises that make it not only difficult to recognize at times, but also difficult to diffuse once it takes hold. It is a vice that begs for secrecy. One can hardly avoid noticing the courageous, at least the heroic ones, but one must search under rocks, around corners, and behind closed doors for the envious. Ironically, this secrecy belies its prevalence, as many note that envy is probably the most common vice across social classes, gender differences, and ages.[3]

Like all the virtues and vices, courage and envy are the ordering and disordering of our desires, which have been habituated over time by a series of wise or poor choices, encouraged by good or bad mentors, or affirmed through socially acceptable patterns of behavior. At first glance, courage and envy make for an odd pairing, for neither is the obvious opposite of the other. The opposite of courage is often considered cowardice, and the opposite of envy is usually deemed love. Then again, our vices and virtues don't always relate as opposites, but rather as each other's enemies whose competition for allegiance in our soul sometimes rests on subtle yet crucial distinctions that are particular to a given culture. I think more can be learned from both of these when we see them as two parts of a hinge. Both envy and courage swing on the center pin of how one relates to the goodness in others. In particular, courage and envy mark the ability or inability to recognize, defend, and celebrate saints and moral exemplars. The courage

2. Olson, *Seven Sins and Seven Virtues*, 21.

3. For a comprehensive study of envy in its cultural, literary, psychological, philosophical, and sociological manifestations, see Schoeck, *Envy: A Theory of Social Behavior*.

to recognize and imitate saints and moral exemplars is something essential to all virtues as they are realized in community.

A Story of Envy: "Greenleaf"

The writer Flannery O'Connor, eminently insightful into how human personalities falter and find grace, brilliantly personifies envy in her short story "Greenleaf." The main character, Mrs. May, is a thin, squint-eyed widow who, for fifteen years, has worked alone at keeping a broken-down farm on the right side of ruin. She never wanted this farm in the first place: she was placed within it by her husband to raise a family, and was bound to it as her sole inheritance upon his death. Mrs. May's only fleeting consolation, as O'Connor describes it, is that "her city friends said she was the most remarkable woman they knew, to go, practically penniless and with no experience, out to a rundown farm and make a success of it. . . . Before any kind of judgment seat, she would be able to say: I've worked, I have not wallowed."[4]

So far, this could be the setup for the story of a strong-willed woman, who courageously worked amid adverse conditions to better her life and the lives of her family. But it is not. Rather, it is a perceptive account of self-destruction brought about by envy and resentment, the very poisons of courage. Mrs. May came into this situation and these obligations before her sense of self had time to mature, and so over time she cultivated a deeprooted envy toward those who seemed free to choose their fate, and eventually toward all those upon whom fortune smiled. As the years went by, and as choice after choice settled the once occasional moments of spite into engrained habits of malice, she eventually could call only one thing her own: her empty resilience over a world that, in her mind, was set to bring her to ruin. "Everything is against you," Mrs. May says, "the weather is against you and the dirt is against you and the help is against you. They're all in league against you!"

Envious people require others on whom to cast their squinting and suspicious glances, living as they do in reaction to the lives others lead. O'Connor provides one such character, Mr. Greenleaf, an African American hired hand who, though legally the employee of Mrs. May, possesses a dignity that elevates him above her spite. Despite his social status as her inferior, he and his family fare well in the world and eventually, to the utter disdain of Mrs. May, become "society." Mrs. May fights a constant and subtle battle against Mr. Greenleaf and his family, seeking any chance possible to

4. O'Connor, *Complete Stories*, 332.

belittle his success or to point out his failings. All along, however, she secretly desires the fortune Mr. Greenleaf has found.

In the end, envy slowly and persistently gnaws at the soul. In the story, O'Connor embodies Mrs. May's envy with a bull, actually the Greenleafs' family bull, which frequently breaks free from its stall and wanders onto Mrs. May's property. Consider how O'Connor describes this bull's invasion of Mrs. May's land, and you will get some idea of how envy infiltrates the soul.

> [As Mrs. May awoke in her bed] she had been conscious in her sleep of a steady rhythmic chewing as if something were eating one wall of the house. She had been aware that whatever it was had been eating as long as she had had the place and had eaten everything from the beginning of her fence line up to the house and now was eating the house and calmly with the same steady rhythm would continue through the house, eating her and the boys, and then on, eating everything but the Greenleafs, on and on, eating everything until nothing was left but the Greenleafs on a little island all their own in the middle of what had been her place.[5]

In light of O'Connor's narrative, we can make a few clarifications about the vice. Envy can become manifest in both individuals and whole communities. We may begin, however, with a straightforward description of the vice within individuals. First, we note that envy is a desire for something that one lacks, but the desiderata of envy can come in endless varietals. You can envy the wisdom of old age if you are young, the vitality of youth if you are old, wealth if you are poor, simplicity if you are wealthy, singlehood if you are married, marriage if you are single, charisma if you are dull, strength if you are weak, etc. But if envy has a definable shape, it is not in the content of what is desired, or even in desperately wanting something you lack. Envy becomes vicious when it turns our desire for anything good into malice toward those who already enjoy what we don't have.

Envy is not jealousy. The two desires press upon the self in structurally different ways. Legitimate jealousy arises within right relationships, when someone's attachment, loyalties, or affections are being usurped by another without just claim. The classic example involves romantic love or contractual marriage. As such, jealousy involves three people: the one experiencing jealousy, the one whose attachments are being directed elsewhere, and the one who has won or taken the affections away from the jealous one. The jealous one may retain within themselves retain a sense of right and

5. Ibid., 312.

superiority compared to the intrusive lover. As such, jealousy leads to two irritations: anger at the rival and anger toward the beloved. While jealousy is nothing terribly admirable, especially when it turns obsessive, it is not, properly speaking, morally problematic in the right circumstances. To make a biblical connection, we can thus appreciate why God is right to be jealous of Israel's devotion to other gods. A wife is rightfully jealous if her husband's affections are imbalanced toward another woman. Neither God nor the jealous spouse necessarily loses their rightful position of strength, for it is the other that has compromised their status.

But envy is different. Envy secretly acknowledges one's own inferiority in the face of the envied, an inferiority that lends such bitterness to malice. Jealousy, properly speaking, does not necessarily seek harm to the other, but rather the restoration of right relationship. Envy, however, destroys the very possibility of relationship between individuals.

Why? Aristotle notes that the noblest pleasure in a virtuous friendship, upon which the best moral communities are founded, is to take joy in the success, beauty, and virtue in one's friend. It recognizes the goodness in one's friend, and never hesitates to lift that up for celebration or admiration. One will courageously defend a friend, precisely because one so freely admires a friend's virtues and seeks to protect and promote their cultivation. Envy, while maybe the most private and interior of the vices, is destructive of such friendships. As Joseph Epstein notes in his book on the subject, *Envy*, "Malice that cannot speak its name, cold-blooded but secret hostility, impotent desire, hidden rancor, and spite all cluster at the center of envy."[6] Friendship becomes impossible to those caged in by envy. For those suffering from *acedia* (sloth), hell is being locked up with oneself; for the envious person, *hell is other people*.

COURAGE: THE ENABLING VIRTUE

From such vice we turn to virtue. No single virtue can be cultivated fully by itself. Some thinkers, Thomas Aquinas in particular, defends the "unity of the virtues" thesis, which states that no virtue can be fully developed without all the virtues being developed. Though I will not go into an analysis of this claim in particular, its intuitive rightness is seen most clearly with courage. We first note that any other virtue requires some degree of courage in order to be realized. For example, how could one become just, if one never had the courage to strive for justice? How could one love, if the resolve necessary to endure mutual suffering with the beloved could not match the

6. Epstein, *Envy*, 7.

fear such suffering evoked? How could one find wisdom, if one didn't have the courage to seek truth amidst a foolish culture? Cornel West remarks in a recent interview filmed in *The Examined Life*, "Courage is *the* enabling virtue for any philosopher, for any human being, in the end. Courage to think. Courage to love. Courage to hope."[7]

We also note that other virtues must be present in order for courage to be considered a *virtue* and not a morally indifferent capacity such as strength or cleverness. When misguided or misapplied, courage becomes downright dangerous to the individual and their community. Without prudence, a courageous soul confidently blunders their way through life, making bold but unwise judgments. Without love, courage leads to the destruction and not protection of relationships. Without temperance, a courageous person cannot balance the courage to act in conflict with the courage to sustain commitments necessary for peace. The virtuous life is of a whole.

Courage to Act: From Achilles to Aristotle

But what is courage and how do we recognize it? Is it bravado? Valor? Daring? Fearlessness? Stalwartness? Aggression? Endurance? How we imagine the virtues and how we grasp their contours is dependent largely upon *who* we assume embodies the virtue. Our exemplars inform our ethics. In the case of courage, it is helpful to begin with the most commonly cited exemplar of courage: the soldier in war. The battlefield has often been the paradigm situation within which one proves one's courage. War and its battles threaten a soldier's physical well-being, drives fear deep into the heart, and demands a decisive action amidst the risk of death. In such situations, a virtuous soldier is the archetype of the *hero*, and the hero's definitive virtue is courage.

Within Western culture, Homer's Achilles serves as the progenitor of this image. Achilles was unmatched in his military prowess as an individual soldier, sense of personal honor, and valor in the face of defending that honor. He was also unmatched is his ability to transform his anger into force, a lethal force that could "storm over the field like a fury, driving all before him, and killing until the earth was a river of blood."[8] Should a king be able to channel Achilles' anger and sense of honor to the benefit of the king's own cause, victory was assured; that is, unless Achilles' *personal courage* triumphed over the courage to fight for the common good or the just cause. The *Illiad*, that "poem of force" as Simone Weil describes it, is precisely a

7. West, quoted in Taylor, *Examined Life*, 6.

8. White, *Radical Virtues*, 17.

tale of the moral ambivalence of Achilles. His individual heroism was awe inspiring to his fellow man, yet it had no bounds outside of his own self-serving ambition for greatness, and only on occasion would it accord with the good of his fellow citizens.

In times of war, we have so often returned to Achilles for the sheer attraction of his heroic personality, even while we have reinterpreted his image over the centuries. Achilles lingered in the cultural memory for the aristocrats in ancient Athens, Caesars in Rome, Medieval knights in the legends of King Arthur, the princes for Machiavelli, revolutionaries in France and America, and even to contemporary corporate CEOs who see business as a competitive battle ground where all spoils can be gained or lost. Achilles' fiercely independent spirit is echoed in the heroes of American Westerns and action movies alike, who all share three key qualities: exceptional skill in killing (when necessary), an anger that can be checked or unleashed at will, and an alienation from society and normal community relations. Within such stories, courage is the virtue of strength and force, of actively conquering the threats to oneself and, in later tellings, one's community.

It should also be noted that according to this telling of cultural myths for the last three thousand years, soldiers and their courage are deemed distinctly masculine. According to the stories our cultures often retell and mythologize, whether they be ancient heroes, chivalrous knights, romantic revolutionaries, stoic cowboys, ostracized police detectives, or corporate raiders reading Sun Tzu's *Art of War* on the airplane flight to their next economic battle, courage is a virtue for men, and men rule through the force of action.

And yet, these are often myopic and nostalgic tellings of the story, harkening back as they do to the hero of a bygone pagan culture that only now exists in myth. It is strange, we must admit, that so many continue to imagine themselves into some version of Achilles.[9]

Another, more compelling way to tell the story is to note how the singular image of courage exemplified in military heroes such as Achilles became increasingly complex over time and, with the decisive influence of Christian culture upon classical culture, changed altogether. To illustrate the evolution of courage, we look to how the militaristic presumptions about courage were challenged by two key thinkers in our history: Aristotle and Aquinas. The challenges both issued are not unique to them, and similar ones have been repeated. The comparison is helpful because Aristotle was

9. Deirdre McCloskey writes, "We, and especially the men among us, keep turning, turning over in our minds aristocratic stories of virtue in the line of the *Iliad*. You would think that bourgeois men of Europe or Japan or America were actual kings of Ithaca, or of Engelond verray, parfit, gentil knights." McCloskey, *Bourgeois Virtues*, 216.

directly influenced by the myth of Achilles, and Aquinas was influenced by Aristotle.

Neither Aristotle nor Aquinas deny the legitimate courage of the soldier that fights for the good cause, but each thinker *re-contextualizes the virtue within a different polity*. Put simply, in contrast to Homeric society, Aristotle attempted to *use* the image of the ideal soldier so that it may be applied among aristocratic statesmen in urban politics. Aquinas, on the other hand, transforms courage altogether by subordinating it to the virtue of love, deeming it a *gift* of the Holy Spirit, and exemplifying it in the martyr. The basic idea is that different politics will produce different virtues. If the *primary* community to which Aquinas belongs is the Church and no longer the Greek city-state, then his virtues should fit *primarily* the ecclesial politic.[10]

Let us begin with Aristotle's attempt to re-imagine the traditional militaristic and glory seeking virtues of Homeric Greece into a urban, democratic, and aristocratic culture. Aristotle knew that the image of Achilles as an exemplar must be overcome if the ideals of Athenian democracy and urban life were to be achieved. Aristotle's argument in the *Nicomachean Ethics* lay in his recognition that courage, like all virtues, required the practical wisdom gained through rational reflection. If a virtue did not engage the rational soul, it was not a *human* virtue. Acting merely from instinct or some primal urge toward violence were not distinctly *human* actions, and thus not exercises in *human* excellences. Thus Aristotle argued that courage required a certain *balance of judgment* between daring and caution, and a certain balance of emotion between audacity and dread. Unlike Achilles' ferocious and unwieldy courage, Aristotle claimed that the person who "faces and fears (or similarly feels confidence about) the right things for the right reasons and in the right way and at the right time is courageous."[11] Such right reasoning and emoting are characterized, according to Aristotle, by a mean between the extremes of cowardice and fearlessness, caution and recklessness. Therefore, courage entails cultivating our ability to *feel, choose, and act* in the right way in light of our *wisdom* of what makes such feelings, choices, and actions accord with the good of the moral community. The emphasis on the *wisdom of the good* necessary for the virtue separates Aristotle's view of courage from Achilles'.

The question remains, who exemplifies this best? Despite his critique of Achilles' immoderate militarism, Aristotle does not leave the image of

10. For a further development of this argument, see Stanley Hauerwas's essay "Courage Exemplified," in *The Hauerwas Reader*.

11. White, *Radical Virtues*, 18.

the soldier behind altogether. For a moral exemplar, he still offers up the image of a soldier facing death in battle as the paradigm of courage. For *death* is the most fearful thing of all, and physical death is precisely what a soldier confronts[12] But it must be a particular kind of death, it must be death in explicit service to a just cause. Facing a natural disaster does not involve as much courage for Aristotle, for one is not *explicitly fighting for a just cause*. A hurricane is not an unjust force, but merely a natural threat. The same would hold true of an individual fighting a disease. In the field of battle, however, the just cause is threatened by an unjust cause—for example, democratic rule of one's own people is threatened by tyrannical rule by a sworn enemy of the city. So the logic follows: fighting for a just cause in the face of threat necessitates courage. In a radical change from Achilles, however, Aristotle claims that sacrificing one's own self for the sake of the common good of one's polis is the height of courage because it is the most honorable kind of death. Courage enables one to actively confront a threat to the *common good* and not just *individual honor*.

Love and the Courage to Endure: From Aristotle to Aquinas

As we know, Thomas Aquinas creatively retrieves much of Aristotle's insights about the nature of the virtues for the purpose of developing a systematic Christian ethic. This influence is especially explicit in his treatment of the cardinal virtues—wisdom, justice, courage and temperance—wherein Aquinas often refers to Aristotle as an authority. Consider, for example, Aquinas's summary of courage and note its similarities to Aristotle's view summarized above.

> Fortitude strengthens a man's mind against the greatest danger, which is that of death. Now fortitude is a virtue; and it is essential to virtue ever to tend to good; wherefore it is in order to pursue some good that man does not fly from the danger of death. But the dangers of death arising out of sickness, storms at sea, attacks from robbers, and the like, do not seem to come on a man through his pursuing some good. On the other hand, the dangers of death which occur in battle come to man directly on account of some good, because, to wit, he is defending the common good by a just fight.[13]

12. Ibid., 20.
13. Aquinas, *Summa Theolgica*, II-II, 123, 5.

Lest we think that Aquinas merely gives Christian legitimacy to Aristotle's moral framework, we must remember that Aquinas' moral theology is also informed foremost by the image of Christ, the message of the Gospels, the Christian theological tradition and the community of saints recognized by his immediate monastic community. Aquinas thus never remains with Aristotle, but ultimately seeks the Christian moral imagination to inform his ethics. We see this first in his subsequent treatment of the kinds of courage deemed virtuous, but ultimately in the kind of exemplar he holds up for imitation.

First, Aquinas notes two types of courage: the courage stemming from a position of strength and manifested in acts of aggression and, the courage stemming from a position of weakness and manifested in acts of endurance. Given the model of courage Christ himself demonstrated, "the principle act of courage is endurance, that is to stand immovable in the face of dangers rather than to attack them."[14] This form of courage, Richard White argues, does not "highlight human strength and virility as do the examples of the ancient Greek warrior or the typical action hero."[15] The courage present in aggressive acts to protect the common good from a tangible threat has its merits when the end and means of such actions are good. Daring courage, Aquinas notes, acts from a position of strength and superiority to the threat. But the courage of endurance is more perfect a virtue because it recognizes our own dependence on divine power, and thus for the faithful can be transformed into a theological virtue.

In her own excellent treatment of Aquinas' ethics, Rebecca DeYoung argues that Aquinas transcends Aristotle not only by recognizing the superior difficulty of endurance over aggression, but by transforming the occasion by which endurance is most recognized. For Aquinas courage is not primarily the soldier, nor the politician, but the martyr who refuses to renounce Christ on pain of death.[16] Now, the image that comes to mind often for Christians is that of a martyr being asked to verbally denounce Christ and swear allegiance to another emperor or god. But certainly the gospels teach us that there are all sorts of ways of renouncing Christ, verbal betrayal being merely one. At its core, the courage of the martyr is motivated by love of neighbor and God. Aquinas spells this out when he considers the question of the Martyr in Question 124, article 3 of the *Summa*:

> Now it is evident that in martyrdom man is firmly strengthened in the good of virtue, since he cleaves to faith and justice

14. Aquinas, *Summa Theologica*, II-II, 123, 6
15. White, *Radical Virtues*, 186.
16. DeYoung, *Glittering Vices*, 185–86.

notwithstanding the threatening danger of death, the immi-
nence of which is moreover due to a kind of particular con-
test with his persecutors. . . . But in the end, martyrdom is a
more perfect manifestation of courage than soldiering in battle
[aggression and daring in the face of fear of death] primarily
because martyrdom is motivated by love (charity). . . . Charity
inclines one to the act of martyrdom, as its first and chief motive cause, being the virtue commanding it, whereas fortitude
inclines thereto as being its proper motive cause, being the
virtue that elicits it. Hence martyrdom is an act of charity as
commanding, and of fortitude as eliciting. For this reason also it
manifests both virtues.

Looking back to Aristotle, we might say that Aristotle directly critiqued his previous culture by situating wisdom above courage in the hierarchy of distinct human excellences. Courage serves wisdom, and for the
Greeks, wisdom is the highest and most distinctly human of the virtues.
Christianity, on the other hand, situated the theological virtue of love above
any of the cardinal virtues. For Christians, courage must serve the ends established by love. Love perfects courage and makes it a human virtue. The
Bible consistently established the priority of love over other virtues, most
explicitly in the Gospels and in Paul's and John's epistles. By the fifth century,
St. Augustine had solidified the theological tradition's prioritization of love,
which continued to be systematically defended leading up to Aquinas in the
thirteenth century. These Christian sources redefined courage not only by
submitting it to the authority of love, but by changing the exemplar of courage away from the solider to the *martyr*. Sociologically speaking, it would
be more correct to say that the exemplar appeared first, which gave rise
to theological and moral recognition of the virtue. The virtue of sacrificial
and self-giving love, for example, is made possible in the moral imagination
because God's own son embodied a way of living worthy of imitation.

In the end, Aquinas' view of courage is based upon the kind of exemplar Christ and the early Christian martyrs gave us more than on the
concept of the virtue itself provided by Aristotle. The lesson here is that *the
kind of exemplar we implore shapes the moral imagination of the virtue itself
and thus the formation of the person.* Aristotle taught the same lesson in his
Ethics, when he defined virtue in terms of that "which the practically wise
person would determine it."[17] We can't define the virtue of courage first, and
then find the exemplar who best represents it. Rather, we must see the exemplar. It matters whether our exemplar is the soldier or the martyr, the hero

17. Aristotle, *Nicomachean Ethics*, II.6:1107.

or the saint. Aristotle re-interpreted the well-worn exemplar of Homer's solider to highlight the role wisdom plays in relation to courage. Aquinas provided another exemplar in the martyr to highlight the role love plays in relation to courage. Courage is the great enabling virtue, Cornel West reminds us. It enables the soldier to defend a city against physical attack, the political leader to defend the common good against foolish decisions, and the martyr to endure great suffering to bear witness to the truth.

We now face a problem neither Aristotle or Aquinas addressed: an envious culture that stymies the very possibility of recognizing moral exemplars at all (heroes or saints). And so in keeping with our story, courage must enable one to overcome envy so that one may be inspired by the saints among us to realize the good.

A CONTEMPORARY THREAT TO VIRTUE

What if envy not only characterized the vices of individual humans, but the basic principles of a society? Envy is most strong between those who share social proximity. It thrives *within* communities more so than *across* communities. To appreciate the communal nature of the vice of envy, we jump ahead six hundred years from Aquinas to the Danish philosopher and Christian thinker Søren Kierkegaard. Among Christian theologians, he is appreciated for his philosophical and psychological brilliance, his critiques of superficial Christian culture, and his edifying discourses on Christian life. His lyrical, ironic, and incisive writing continue to provoke contemporary Christians to self-examination.

Kierkegaard develops a description of the envious society in a brief review of a nineteenth-century novel, *The Present Age*. Kierkegaard's diagnosis of his society goes something like this. By the middle of the nineteenth century, Denmark became a modern nation with a rising middle class, the emergence of laissez-faire economics, freedom of the press, and a stable constitutional monarchy. The influence of the clergy on society was steadily being replaced by the nobility, professors, scientists, and businessmen. And so these Danish Christians, for all Danes were "Christians" since baptism was required for citizenship, settled into the quiet comforts and undemanding lifestyles of the middle class, where their most pressing obligation was to manage their debts. As such, they suffered typical diseases of the middle class: boredom and envy.[18] Kierkegaard's critiques of his society offered foresight into the superficiality of many communities within contemporary

18. For an analysis of Kierkegaard's critique of this description of Danish society, see Elrod, "Passion, Reflection, and Particularity."

affluent Western countries. Unlike much of the writing on envy in the High Middle Ages, including both Dante and Aquinas, Kierkegaard considers envy a social phenomenon.

According to Kierkegaard, any society that hopes to encourage enduring moral character and authentic religious inwardness must have the ability to *admire greatness* by recognizing, without resentment, individual exemplars and saints. While this idea was nothing new, Kierkegaard saw it threatened through an increasing suspicion of the very idea of saintliness in moral and religious life. The admiration of saints and heroes is so essential because, according to Kierkegaard, "what usually happens where admiration is authentic is that the admirer is inspired by the thought of being a person just like the distinguished one, is humbled by the awareness of not having been able to accomplish this great thing himself, is ethically encouraged by the prototype to follow this exceptional man's example to the best of his ability."[19] Virtuous admiration requires both the recognition of the greatness of the exemplar, and the recognition of one *not being the exemplar.* And yet, one does not get lost in despair for oneself, or resentful toward the blessed one, but one takes hope and encouragement that imitation is still possible and that over time, *with work*, one may grow into the role.

Without moral exemplars and saintly individuals whom we both esteem and tremble before, moral communities would flounder. Exemplars are the recognized personification of a community's virtues and values. It is not the case that the admirer wants to be the esteemed individual—for example, I don't want to be St. Francis, but I want to live into the virtues and ideals that St. Francis embodied. "The admirers are held together in the ethical relation for each participates in the relation to the ideal, a deed or the achievement of moral excellence. This is good glue for society."[20] Kierkegaard believes that in modern middle-class life, the courage it takes to truly admire another has been lost on a societal level. "No one is any longer carried away by the desire for the good to perform *great* things, no one is precipitated by evil into atrocious sins, and so there is nothing for either the good or the bad to talk about, and yet for that very reason people gossip all the more, since ambiguity is tremendously stimulating and much more verbose than rejoicing over goodness or repentance over evil."[21]

Today we might describe this in terms of the difference between envy and emulation. Young writers rightfully emulate those they consider brilliant, creative, or skilled. Athletes are pushed to higher achievements

---

19. Kierkegaard, *Two Ages,* 72.
20. Ibid.
21. Kierkegaard, *Present Age,* 42.

by their competitors without seeking their competitors' demise. Hulmut Schoeck, in his comprehensive analysis of envy, offers up the example of two runners in a race. If for much of the race, one runner is lagging behind another, she may seek to emulate her competitor as she strives to achieve what her competitor is accomplishing. Properly speaking, she who emulates another would never wish the downfall of the other, but rather the other's perfection of talent, against which the emulator could also be spurred to achieve as well. When healthy, emulation allows two athletes to raise the level of the game for both. In contrast, as we saw with Flannery O'Connor's character, Ms. May, envy seeks equality by tearing down the other, tripping the competitor before the finish line, or hoping one's rival pulls a hamstring along the way.

Dorothy Sayers notes the *leveling* that envy promotes: "Envy is the great leveler: if it cannot level things up, it will level them down. . . . At its best, envy is a climber and a snob; at its worst it is a destroyer—rather than have anyone happier than itself, it will see us all miserable together."[22] Kierkegaard cites several examples of this leveling, more fitting perhaps in his own time, though we could imagine our own more contemporary versions of this issue. Without the recognition of the qualitative difference, daughters and sons don't understand what it would mean to grow and mature into exemplary parents, apprentices don't learn from masters, and young Christians don't earnestly strive to imitate the exemplary saints that have come before them. Instead, they precociously and prematurely claim equality with their would be exemplars.

Ultimately, Kierkegaard holds, the refusal to acknowledge qualitative differences within one's moral community translates into a destruction of the God-human relation. Robert Perkins summarizes Kierkegaard's critique by noting that when people are incapable of living for an ideal, and refuse to recognize the qualitative difference of the exemplars in their community,

> then persons relate to each other simply *en masse*. The result is violence, anarchy, barbarism, decadence, gossip, rumor, and an apathetic envy that becomes the standard in human relations. Persons have nothing else to look at except each other, and they turn on each other in suspicion and aggression. The wretchedness is caused by the fact that there is nothing more important than their own petty little selves to talk to and think about. There is no passion for anything, including themselves. Social relationships become envious; talk becomes chatter; thinking becomes public opinion; right and duty become self-serving prudence;

22. Sayers, *Letters to a Diminished Church*, 94.

neighbor-love becomes a demand by the neighbor; the aesthetic becomes entertainment; political thought and policy formation become polls. The only relief from boredom is envy.[23]

In the end, envy prevents a fundamental kind of courage: the courage to recognize the exemplars among the saints without threat, the courage to know one's own limitations without fear, and the courage to commit to an ideal and endure the suffering necessary to embody the good. Whereas for Dante and Aquinas, the opposite of envy could be generosity, the opposite disposition to envy as a social phenomenon is *right admiration*. Certainly, no human exemplar should be divinized into Christ himself, for all have fallen short. Envy's only alterative, however, is to demonize those worthy of our emulation. Kierkegaard's insight is neither communalism nor authoritarianism. Rather, it is the way in which moral maturation is possible in society. Each person finds their individuality in relation to that which they admire, which is always something other than their own individual self. By finding an ideal for which to live, each individual has their own task before them, which may be exemplified in the virtuous other. Through the mutual recognition of this ideal, communities of individuals relate to one another through a mutual commitment to a common cause and shared admiration for those who best embody that ideal. Without this courage, virtue cannot be recognized or achieved.

Vulnerability and Fear

Courage in the Christian tradition is not morally ambiguous. As a *virtue*, it is an excellence of character worthy of praise. This means that courage is not merely a human capacity (like strength) nor merely an emotion (like self-confidence). As an excellence of moral character that is cultivated over time through habit, courage stems originally from an acute awareness of human vulnerability, the appropriate fear of evil or harm to one's own self, and the choice to act decisively on behalf of a just and good cause.

The courage a particular moral community needs depends on the threat to the good of that community. In a culture threatened by tangible dangers, we must find the courage to act decisively to *actively resist* those threats. Aristotle has much to teach us here. In a culture threatened by unrelenting sufferings, we must find the courage to *endure those sufferings* in a way that bears witness to the truth and encourages hope. Here, Aquinas is a helpful guide. In a culture threatened by superficiality and decadence, we

23. Perkins, "Envy," 117.

must find the courage once again to commit to the goodness beyond each of us, admire the saints who have come before us and are among us, and strive for humility and ultimately love.

Joseph Pieper writes that courage "presumes vulnerability . . . to be brave means to be ready to sustain a wound."[24] The invincible do not require courage, whereas the truly brave realize all too well that the wound they risk receiving when they enter the fray is an evil. Though the heart of courage is being prepared to die for the just cause, the courageous person neither loves death nor despises life. The envious, on the other hand, can indeed despise life and savor the wounds they inflict on themselves, to the point even, as we see in the climax of the story "Greenleaf," of relishing death itself. A clever way to note the difference between the envious and courageous is that the envious love to "play the martyr," publicly amplifying their wounds to evoke pity in others, while the courageous truly are martyrs, deflecting their suffering to point to the good, to God. To have the courage of a martyr is to be ready to suffer for the sake of the highest reality, and then to forego even the heroic.

The crucial difference between a pagan conception of moral virtue and a Christian one is the difference between being moral heroes and moral saints. For the Christian, saintly courage always points away from the self and toward God. To be brave is not to be without fear. In the horrors of life's battles, only the foolhardy think there is no reason to fear, and thus they rush headlong into danger. Only those who have lost the will to live and have foregone any attachments to persons and place in this life have no fear of death. Courage, then, *fears appropriately.* To that extent, the courageous person *is* afraid of evil, but does not allow him or herself to be drawn by fear away from the just cause he or she seeks to accomplish.

Conclusion

In conclusion then, we can consider how the cultivation of courage bulwarks the soul against envy. Both envy and courage hinge on how one relates one's self to the goodness in others. They are both other-oriented moral perspectives. Envious persons desperately long for a self they lack. But they don't allow themselves to admire the gifts of others who might then inspire them to become better, nor do they sacrifice their own desires for the sake of bettering another. The courageous person makes the reverse movement and realizes that virtue comes from risking one's self, in the face of a real threat, for the sake of the friend, the neighbor, and ultimately God. The truly

24. Pieper, *Virtues of the Human Heart*, 24.

courageous possess an acute awareness of their gifts and vulnerabilities, and are admirable in the face of this, because they risk being wounded for the sake of something else worthy of praise.

In Philippians 1:15–20, Paul indicates the difference between courage and envy. "It is true that some preach Christ out of envy and rivalry, but others out of goodwill. The latter do so out of love, knowing that I am put here for the defense of the gospel. The former preach Christ out of selfish ambition, not sincerely, supposing that they can stir up trouble for me while I am in chains. But what does it matter? The important thing is that in every way, whether from false motives or true, Christ is preached. And because of this I rejoice. . . . I eagerly expect and hope that I will in no way be ashamed, but will have sufficient courage so that now as always Christ will be exalted in my body, whether by life or by death" (TNIV).

7

ON BEING RECONCILED
Anger and Justice

IN DECEMBER 1955, ROSA Parks, Martin Luther King Jr., Ralph Abernathy, and the citizens of Montgomery, Alabama, boycotted the city's bus lines to protest the rampant segregation and oppression of blacks in the city. In King's autobiographical account of the events, *Stride Toward Freedom*, he describes those crucial first days of the boycott, when the tensions of hope and apprehension permeated the deliberations of the protestors and city officials alike. On December 18, less than two weeks after the boycott began, King went to the city council to speak on behalf of the black delegation, hopeful that an early solution might be reached. Upon entering the meeting, however, he quickly noticed that among the city officials were members of the racist White Citizens Council. King spoke out on behalf of his fellow citizens, only to be publicly defamed by the council itself. The white city council pulled out of the negotiations, and the hope for an early solution was dashed. The boycott and the difficulties this imposed on African Americans in Montgomery, would last another year.

King returned home that night. In his own words, he arrived home with a "heavy heart. I was weighted down by a terrible sense of guilt, remembering that on two or three occasions I had allowed myself to become angry and indignant. . . . 'You must not harbor anger,' I admonished myself.

'You must be willing to suffer the anger of the opponent, and yet not return anger.'[1] Not return anger against such hate? How can we make sense of King's feeling of guilt for allowing himself to become angry in the face of such injustice? And yet, throughout his ministry and civil rights work, King would speak often about his struggles with anger. He would later write,

> The discontent is so deep, the anger so ingrained, the despair, the restlessness so wide, that something has to be brought into being to serve as a channel through which these deep emotional feelings, these deep angry feelings, can be funneled. . . . I see this campaign [of nonviolent resistance] as a way to transmute the inchoate rage of the ghetto into a constructive and creative channel.[2]

In the last chapter, I examined the need for courage to recognize and imitate saintly exemplars. Martin Luther King Jr. was certainly one of those worthy of imitation, and if even he worried over the destructiveness of anger, then we should probably take note.

King's saintly courage amidst hatred raises a question for us. In a world where injustice too often gets the upper hand, where the little rain that falls on the fields of the just gets so easily diverted to the already rich top soils of the unjust, why shouldn't those who are oppressed lash out in anger against their oppressors? How else do the abused and disenfranchised resist the powerful, except with power? Anger feels like power. Anger feels like righteousness. It often feels like justice itself. But it isn't, and the wise person understands the crucial difference between a virtue and its perversion into a vice.

In this chapter, we examine our final pairing: anger and justice. It is necessary to appreciate the complexities of these character traits so that we may live better in light of divine grace. Exaggerating the differences between virtues and vices does not help us advance grace toward the real people that wrestle with them. And so, as we did with each of the previous vices and virtues, we are looking for the hinge upon which these two swing. The hinge is some basic human capacity that operates in the moral life. That capacity can be developed to contribute to one's flourishing or one's debasement. As well shall see below, the pin upon which anger and justice swing is in how we *respond* to the systematic sins that pervade our world.

Anger is a complex vice to figure out for another reason. When reading the biblical texts on anger, it is not easy to get a clear picture of anger as a vice when we are reminded to fear the wrath of God in one passage and

---

1. King, *Stride Toward Freedom*, 110.
2. King, "Showdown for Nonviolence," in *Testament of Hope*, 69.

to resist anger in another. In his recent book on the vice, Robert Thurman notes that in the Old Testament, "the angriest person around seems to be God himself."[3] From the curses God sets upon Adam, Eve, and Cain, to cleansing the corrupt earth with a flood, to hardening Pharaoh's heart, to killing the Egyptians' firstborn, God gets angry at humans again and again. How can we we reconcile the destructive potential of the vice with the divine attribute of wrath?

FROM EMOTION TO VICE

To begin, we may note three kinds of anger: anger as an emotion, anger as a vice directed toward a particular person or polity, and holy anger, sometimes called righteous indignation. Each has its own relation to the virtue of justice.

As a mere emotion, or *passion* as theologians would name it, anger entails the agitation aroused occasionally by the insults, slights, and injustices we experience. Such emotions wax and wane according to the particularities of personalities and the severity of the offenses endured. Anger, however, goes beyond mere frustration or agitation. For the classic and medieval authors, Aristotle offered a standard description of the causes and motivations behind this emotion. In typical fashion, Aristotle begins with a definition. "Anger may be defined as an impulse, accompanied by pain, to a conspicuous revenge for a conspicuous slight directed without justification towards what concerns oneself or towards what concerns one's friends."[4]

We may note several aspects of Aristotle's view of anger. First, anger often stems from wounded pride, which itself stems from a kind of aggrandized self-importance that others fail to publically recognize. It is important to note that as insightful as Aristotle is about the psychology of anger, he himself writes as an aristocrat within an honor-based culture. In such a context, one's publically acknowledge rank, position, and status are paramount to one's own worth. Naturally then, a "conspicuous slight" is a key cause of anger for him. The original harm done by a slight comes in three forms: contempt, spite, and insolence. The offending other may show contempt for something that is of importance to me. The other may also deliberately thwart my desires or plans though it benefits nobody—i.e., spite. Finally, the other may show insolence to me, whereby they conspicuously shame me, mock me, or fail to give me my due honor.[5]

3. Thurman, *Anger*, 32.
4. Aristotle, *Rhetoric*, 1380.
5. Ibid., 1382.

The second thing we note in Aristotle's definition is that anger is an emotion that disposes one to *action*. Sure, some may stew in their anger, bottle it up, or themselves be consumed by it. At its root, however, anger presses one to act, and to act with a particular motivation: revenge! As such, anger is a *derivative* emotion, unlike, say, the emotion of pride, which may well up within oneself. Anger is a reaction, a response, a reply to a "conspicuous slight without justification." Its primary motivation, revenge, is thus also a re-action to something prior. Note the synonyms of *revenge*: *retribution* and *retaliation*. Like *revenge*, each of these begins with the Latin prefix "re-" (again). The revenge that anger seeks is an impulse to *repeat* a harm in light of an original harm done.

The third thing we note in Aristotle's definition of anger is its inherent social dimension. Revenge is always directed at some person or group of persons considered responsible for the harm. Anger requires a guilty party or, if one cannot be found legitimately, a scapegoat. Aristotle doesn't think that anger can be properly directed toward something impersonal like bad weather or even disease. By its nature, anger compels us to find some personal or divine agent responsible. "Why does *God* send tornadoes?" "If the *doctors* would have only diagnosed the cancer earlier, she might have lived." "Our marriage was going along just fine, if *he* did not have to do that!" Anger is also social, interestingly, because it can be experienced on behalf of someone else. Aristotle claims that the original harm that provoked my anger could just as easily been done to my friend as to me. In keeping with Aristotle's view of friendship, this transference is to be expected. In a virtuous friendship, I and my friend become one soul in two bodies. When my friend is honored, so am I, and vice-versa. To dishonor or harm my friend is to dishonor or harm me. Lastly, anger is a social virtue because the slight or harm is *publicly* known. Aristotle is insightful to highlight the "conspicuous" character of anger, revenge, and the antecedent slight. Much anger can be rooted in having been shamed, and desiring to shame in return. The shaming that so easily provokes vicious anger is necessarily conspicuous, and thus the retaliatory impulse also cries out to be conspicuous. Like all emotions, anger may seem to be a private matter but is indeed social.

The last element of anger that Aristotle's definition notes is that while an experience of pain always accompanies anger, anger is also accompanied by a particular pleasure. "[Anger] is also attended by a certain pleasure because the thoughts dwell upon the act of vengeance, and the images then called up cause pleasure, like the images called up in dreams."[6] Revenge, the angry person feels, will be *sweet*. Certainly since the time of Aristotle,

6. Ibid., 1380.

running through Shakespeare's poetry, and to the present day, people have referenced the *sweetness* of revenge. In fact, in a study published in the journal *Science*, scientists demonstrated the neurological manifestations of revenge's sweetness. As the brain studies show, vengeful desire is driven by the anticipated pleasure one will experience when punishing bad behavior in others. As Aristotle named twenty-five hundred years ago and our neuroscientists do today, we experience anger as a kind of dream-like state— whereby the *imagined* completion of some act of revenge offers a unique pleasure.

ANGER AS A VICE

A virtue or vice is a settled disposition cultivated over time through habit that encourages (in the case of virtue) or discourages (in the case of vice) praiseworthy actions. The virtuous person would be expected to experience anger emotionally in the face of injustice, but she would be oriented toward it in the appropriate way, in response to the appropriate offense, to an appropriate degree, for the appropriate amount of time. *As a vice, anger is defined by the disposition to return violence with violence, to enact wrath and revenge upon those particular people who have wronged one, and to sever as far as possible the relationship between oneself and those deemed blameworthy.* This is no mere emotion of anger, but rather a consuming desire for vengeance that comes to define one's character. At its peak, vicious anger entails three elements: a felt judgment of guilt upon the offending other, a misplaced emphasis on one's own innocence, and a desire for the others' destruction at all cost. Aquinas clarifies the situation when anger moves from being a mere passion to a vice.

> The movement of anger may be inordinate and sinful in two ways. First, on the part of *the appetible object*, as when one desires unjust revenge; and thus anger is a mortal sin in the point of its genus, because it is contrary to charity and justice. . . . Secondly, the movement of anger may be inordinate in *the mode of being angry*, for instance, if one be too fiercely angry inwardly, or if one exceed in the outward signs of anger. On this way anger is not a mortal sin in the point of its genus; yet it may happen to be a mortal sin, for instance if through the fierceness of his anger a man fall away from the love of God and his neighbor.[7]

7. Aquinas, *Summa Theologia*, II-II, 158, 3.

Though examples of vicious anger abound in the stories of any culture, I offer up a brief example from Shakespeare's play *Coriolanus* based on his reading of Plutarch's own historical account of the Roman ruler. Caius Marcius Coriolanus is a legendary Roman hero from the fifth century BC. He was truly a proud man and considered himself, not without some reason, better than all other Romans. For his success and unsurpassed courage in battle, Rome's noblemen desire to honor Coriolanus by making him a political representative of the common people of Rome. His fellow countrymen, Sicinius and Brutus, however, fear his unchecked power and popularity. In turn, they sway the common people to condemn Coriolanus to an unmerited death sentence. A lifetime of soldiering is not often a good preparation for domestic politics. Coriolanus becomes rightly enraged at such injustice against him, but has no political or personal virtues or wisdom to do anything but seek vengeance upon Sicinius, Brutus, and indeed, all Romans. He is subsequently banished from the city. Consumed by his anger, he flees to the city of Rome's enemy and helps them plot to seize Rome and defeat the empire. In the most compelling scene in the play, Coriolanus arrives at the encampment of Rome's enemies and offers to his enemy his own wrath and desire for vengeance against his homeland for his enemies to use as they see fit. He speaks to his former enemies, now allies in vengeance, of the betrayal he suffered and revenge he seeks.

> The cruelty and envy of the people,
> Permitted by our dastard nobles, who
> Have all forsook me, hath devour'd the rest;
> And suffer'd me by the voice of slaves to be
> Whoop'd out of Rome. Now this extremity
> Hath brought me to thy hearth; not out of hope—
> Mistake me not—to save my life, for if
> I had fear'd death, of all the men i' the world
> I would have 'voided thee, but in mere spite,
> To be full quit of those my banishers,
> Stand I before thee here. Then if thou hast
> A heart of wreak in thee, that wilt revenge
> Thine own particular wrongs and stop those maims
> Of shame seen through thy country, speed thee straight,
> And make my misery serve thy turn: so use it
> That my revengeful services may prove
> As benefits to thee, for I will fight
> Against my canker'd country with the spleen
> Of all the under fiends.[8]

8. *Coriolanus*, IV.v, lines 80–98.

Coriolanus's emotional anger at his own people was justified, though it need not have become vicious. But with a moral imagination formed solely by retributive justice, he had no desire to transform his wrath into anything other than destruction of his betrayers. His vicious rage became its own end, so much so that it could be hired out against his own people. His identity within any human family, community, or polity at this point was lost. As he states in a later scene, "Wife, mother, child, I know not. My affairs are servanted to others."

The logic of vicious anger is not simply to inflict harm "measure for measure" against the offender. Revenge goes beyond a reciprocal response for the harm done, because it desires to inflict an additional harm to rectify the *offense* for the *unjustified* character of the original harm. In seeking some direct harm proportional to the offense, it necessarily escalates the violence. Theologian Miroslav Volf writes, "Revenge doesn't say, 'An eye for an eye.' It says, 'You take my eye, and I'll blow out your brains.' . . . It doesn't say, 'You organize an act of terror, and we'll punish you.' It says, You organize an act of terror, and we'll use the overwhelming military force of a superpower to recast the political landscape of the entire region from which you came."[9] In the end, anger lays waste to the possibility of redemption by so limiting the moral imagination that the wrathful become nothing more than swords, wielded without reflection or remorse. Anger is thus the deadliest of sins.

FROM ANGER TO JUSTICE

In contrast to Shakespeare's *Coriolanus*, we read Psalm 9. This Psalm is, by no means, an isolated appeal to God's mercy, patience, and forgiveness in the face of anger. We read exhortations against anger throughout the Scriptures—in other Psalms, Proverbs, in Paul's letters, and from Christ himself in the Gospels. But Psalm 9 is one of those helpful passages that seems to contain the whole of the gospel message within it.

> Bless the Lord, O my soul, and all that is within me,
> bless his holy name.
> Bless the Lord, O my soul, and do not forget all his benefits—
> who forgives all your iniquity, who heals all your diseases,
> who redeems your life from the Pit,
> who crowns you with steadfast love and mercy,
> who satisfies you with good as long as you live
> so that your youth is renewed like the eagle's.

9. Volf, *Free of Charge*, 159

The Lord works vindication and justice for all who are oppressed.

He made known his ways to Moses, his acts to the people of Israel.

The Lord is merciful and gracious,
slow to anger and abounding in steadfast love.

He will not always accuse, nor will he keep his anger for ever.

He does not deal with us according to our sins,
nor repay us according to our iniquities.

For as the heavens are high above the earth,
so great is his steadfast love towards those who fear him;

as far as the east is from the west,
so far he removes our transgressions from us.

As a father has compassion for his children,
so the Lord has compassion for those who fear him.

For he knows how we were made; he remembers that we are dust.

In the middle of this Psalm—set within praise of God's patience, forgiveness, and steadfast love—is the passage: "The Lord works vindication
and justice for all those who are oppressed." We turn now to the connection
between justice, anger, and forgiveness noted here. So far in this chapter,
justice has been in the background of our examination of anger. As we
noted in the beginning of the chapter, anger itself can seem like justice. If
anger is caused by a conspicuous slight, offence, or harm, then it would
seem that anger demands justice. "Its not fair!" the protestor shouts to the
powers. What would a demand for justice be, if it wasn't angry? And yet, in
Psalm 9 we see that God both works justice and is slow to anger and repays
not our own inequities. Though absurd to even compare the two, whereas
Coriolanus has no storehouses of mercy or forgiveness within him to act
differently, God overflows with steadfast love and mercy.

The intellectual work of reimagining God's justice, and even God's
anger, is helped by considering the general philosophical view of justice. In
the philosophical tradition, stemming from Plato and continuing through
to contemporary political philosopher John Rawls, justice is the supreme
virtue of social institutions and polities. Justice has also been recognized as
a virtue of individual persons, in both philosophical and theological traditions. Thus, both institutions and individual moral agents can be just or
unjust. With regard to institutions, there are a host of types of justice—legal,
procedural, distributive, retributive, restorative, and social justice. To simplify, there are two basic forms of justice in institutions: legal justice and
social justice. Legal justice mandates procedural fairness in treating people

in their standing before the law with regard to the just establishment of law, the treatment of those alleged or guilty of breaking the law, and the arbitration of disputes between parties. Social justice, by contrast, refers to the "fairness" or "rightness" of the overall distribution of benefits and burdens in society that result from social cooperation. Broadly speaking, both forms of justice are appropriated within Christian theological traditions as components of good communities.

While the questions regarding social justice are ancient, the contemporary term "social justice" is operative across both Christian communities and secular political movements. The contemporary term has been shaped by two Christian movements begun in the later nineteenth century: The Protestant Social Gospel Movement and the early writings of Catholic Social Thought. Both of these were direct responses to the problems distinct to social upheavals and mass urban poverty resulting from the Industrial Revolution. And so, the contemporary connotations of social justice link back to its emergence in nineteenth-century urban settings, reflect issues of power, privilege, and wealth, and focus particularly on those groups within society that lack these benefits. This legacy is seen in the most important twentieth-century contribution to a secular theory of justice from John Rawls, who explicitly states that a necessary condition for a just change in society be that it benefit those who suffer the most injustice, as well as in the work of one of the most effective practitioners and visionaries of social justice, Martin Luther King Jr. As it adopts the language of the New Testament, social justice in its current valuation focuses on "the least of these." In the language of Catholic Social Thought, there is a "preferential option for the poor" inherent in social justice.

Justice is often seen to be a virtue more descriptive of societies and less of individuals. It is the ruling consensus of contemporary social and political theorists that an individual virtue of justice is redundant if the institutional virtue of justice defining a community or society is in place. Much more attention is thus given to articulating a just society than a just person.[10] Such thinking might dictate, for example, that as long as there is systematic justice that guarantees liberties, equality, and a just distribution of power and benefits, compassion and friendship are necessary personal virtues, but justice is not. In addition, some social-justice advocates so emphasize the need for systemic change in society around issues like racism, economic inequality, or immigration reform that they fail to see the importance of cultivating one's own virtue in the individual soul alongside such systemic

10. White, *Radical Virtues*, 89.

efforts. This conception among philosophers, political theorists, or activists is not, however, in keeping with a Christian conception of the virtues.

JUSTICE IN THE UNIVERSAL AND PARTICULAR

From a Christian theological perspective, there is no stark separation between individual and community. Each individual is made in the image of God, and that image of God is made manifest in how one lives in community with others. The Christian God itself is a community of love between three persons that informs what it means to be made in the image of God. The twofold commandment to love God and neighbor acknowledges that to love God is to love *what* God loves and *how* God loves them. As such, we practice justice as a virtue as much in our individual relationships as we do in the larger society. Richard White notes,

> For justice to prevail anywhere, it's not enough to have a perfect legal system or a set of correct policies in place, for even if the laws are just, it does not follow that the people are just or will become just in the course of time. . . . Those who struggle for justice in the world often [do so] against impossible odds. . . . We celebrate these heroes who are devoted to justice, as individual exemplars of virtue whose lives are worthy of imitation.[11]

In this chapter, we focus on virtue as it exists in the intersection of the personal and the political, the individual and the community, the child of God and His church. For justice is fundamentally a social virtue that is embodied in our particular relationships with particular people.

Going deeper into the distinctive character of a Christian theological notion of justice, we highlight two biblical features of the virtue: shalom and covenant. Shalom is the Hebrew word denoting peace, but connoting holistic harmony, health, well-being, and flourishing of right relationship between God and humanity, humanity with each other, and indeed both with the earth. Shalom is holistic with regard to the life of the human person—body, mind, soul—and the human politic, within which each person lives—from children to elders, poor to rich, ruled to rulers. Shalom thus points to a state of affairs within which God's purposes for humanity are lived out and not disrupted by the power structures and struggles within a person or a community.

Justice, in a biblical sense, is also rooted in the idea of *covenant*. That is, justice does not merely aim at *shalom* as a state of affairs, but entails an

11. Ibid., 90.

ongoing, explicit, and committed relationship over time between God and humanity. As covenantal, justice makes known what each party can expect from the other and to whom each is called to be loyal. It also establishes stability overtime through the evocation and execution of just laws and mutual responsibilities. Such laws and mutual responsibilities wed the *law*, or legislation, to justice. Living in accordance with just laws enables a community to better live toward shalom, but this is only part of the story. In the end, justice itself must become a virtue of the human heart.

Along these lines, one of the first things a just person must acknowledge is that no system of justice, no right collection of laws expertly crafted and deftly executed, no architecture of punishment to house offenders, achieves shalom. Josef Pieper critiques the idea that some *system* of distributive justice could be designed to solve the problems of injustice: "If the basic act of commutative justice is called 're-stitution,' the very word implies that it is never possible for men to realize an ideal and definitive condition. What it means is, rather, that the fundamental condition of man and his world is provisory, temporary, nondefinitive, tentative."[12] By all means, laws and structures are needed to give space for right relationships to flourish and not self-destruct. But precisely because the shalom that justice seeks is *relational*, it must be *responsive* to the particular others we live and suffer, each of whom has a dignity distinct from the system. Justice must be able to improvise on love's demands playing out between those with whom I am bound. And those to whom I am bound are always particular people, not ideal types. To the extent that a well designed and intentioned system of justice forgets this, it quickly fails to honor the humanity of the people it aims to serve. This is where justice as a personal virtue comes into play beyond all the necessary just laws that communities may uphold. "The just man, the more he realizes that he is the recipient of gifts and that he has an obligation to God and to man, will alone be ready to fulfill what he does not owe. He will decide to give something to the other that no-one can force him to give."[13]

Given what we have said so far, we may offer a working definition of the virtue of justice to make our point about anger more clearly. *Justice is the virtue that inclines us to live in right relationship to other people and to structure societies wherein imperfect individuals can covenant together not only fairly, but in ways that make forgiveness between individuals possible and that foster shalom among them.* In a fallen world, justice is fundamentally *restorative* of our relationships gone awry. This side of heaven, relationships

12. Pieper, *Four Cardinal Virtues*, 80.
13. Ibid., 26.

between individuals and peoples will always need mending. The meaning of justice as a virtue of the people of God only makes sense in the context of the ongoing work of grace and redemption through Christ, who makes justice possible, both as an exemplar and as the author of creation itself. Again, we see how a Christian conception of grace transforms the Greek virtues tradition.

REIMAGINING ANGER THROUGH JUSTICE

Consider again our opening illustration, which recounts the justified anger of African Americans who have been, and continue to be, deeply wronged by centuries of oppression. Imagine other scenarios of injustice: a Jew in 1938 Germany, an Anabaptist in the sixteenth century, a woman in an abusive marriage, a gay man disowned from his family, a person who has been wrongfully defamed or imprisoned, an immigrant denied their dignity. In each of these we look to the meaning of justice offered by the Christian tradition as a restorative and redemptive movement that seeks to work through the emotion of anger toward reconciliation. Justice does not deny the legitimacy of the emotion or even judgment of anger. The virtue of justice, however, doesn't let anger get the upper hand on its movement toward reconciliation. Justice redeems anger.

One of the central tasks of King's nonviolent movement for civil rights and the vision for the beloved community is to transform the justified anger of those suffering injustice into a creative force. During the Montgomery bus boycott, in 1954, King wrote, "The discontent is so deep, the anger so ingrained, the despair, the restlessness so wide, that something has to be brought into being to serve as a channel through which these deep emotional feelings, these deep angry feelings, can be funneled. . . . I see this campaign [of nonviolent resistance] as a way to transmute the inchoate rage of the ghetto into a constructive and creative channel."[14] In reflections on his predecessor Dr. Du Bois, King wrote, in 1968, "Above all, [Du Bois] did not content himself with hurling invectives for emotional release and then to retire into smug passive satisfaction. History had taught him it is not enough for people to be angry—*the supreme task [of a leader] is to organize and unite people so that their anger becomes a transforming force.*"[15] How is this done?

The first characteristic of a justice that re-imagines anger is that it "allow suffering to speak." Legitimate anger opens a space from which

14. King, "Showdown for Nonviolence," in *Testament of Hope*, 69.
15. King, "Honoring Dr. Du Bois," 36.

truth may be uncovered. Dr. Du Bois, Rev. Dr. King, and in the same line of Christian thinkers, Dr. Cornel West, understand that anger cannot be ignored, left to boil under a sealed pot, or wished away with naïve optimism. The Christian tradition claims that the anger of those who suffer injustice must be transformed creatively by the virtues of justice and love. Cornel West explains this elegantly through the metaphor of the Blues.

> The Bluesman or Blueswoman begins with the catastrophic. You see, the Blues is the autobiographical chronicle of personal catastrophe expressed lyrically. It's a lyrical response to the monstrous. . . . The situation of poor people is catastrophic—Black people had slavery, Jim Crow, Jane Crow, catastrophic! What was their response? It was not to create a Black al-Qaeda, it wasn't counter-terroristic. In the face of slavery, Frederick Douglass said what? "With a smile, and wounds, we want to create freedom for everyone else, we don't want to enslave others just as we were enslaved. Jim Crow? We have no rights and liberties, we are civically dead, we don't want to Jim Crow someone else. We want rights and liberties for everybody. The Bluesman [not simply as a form of music, but the underlying way of life the music represents] responds to the catastrophic with compassion, without drinking from the cup of bitterness, not with revenge but with justice.[16]

Upon giving the oppressed a voice to speak their suffering, the second condition for restorative justice is to reimagine anger. Vicious anger can be transformed into a *holy anger* that resists vicious anger's devolution into hatred, bitterness, and alienation. Holy anger is not so much a virtue itself, but rather makes possible the movement of justice. In thinking back on one of the darkest moments of his life—the night his home was bombed—King offers up this reflection.

> While I lay in that quiet front bedroom, with a distant street lamp throwing a reassuring glow through the curtained window, I began to think of the viciousness of people who would bomb my home. I could feel the anger rising when I realized that my wife and baby could have been killed. I thought about the city commissioners and all the statements that they had made about me and the Negro generally. I was once more on the verge of corroding hatred. And once more I caught myself and said: "You must not allow yourself to become bitter."[17]

16. West, "Catastrophic Love."
17. King, *Stride Toward Freedom*, 110.

Lest this passage seem to indicate a denial of anger, note that the anger that King resists is the kind of anger wed to "hatred" and "bitterness." These forms of anger are so poisonous because they terminate relationship and the hope for reconciliation.

In her book *Holy Anger*, biblical scholar Lytta Basset examines three exemplars—Jacob, Job, and Jesus—to uncover an alternative to the anger leading to hatred, bitterness, and alienation. She takes the word *holy* as key. Holy anger *separates* us from a host of destructive and vicious alternatives.

Holy anger separates us from the cycle of revenge. Holy anger does not seek to control vengeance, though it does not deny the wrongs suffered or the pain endured. Holy anger realizes that broken relationship is punishment enough, and thus does not seek to take vengeance into one's own hands by doing further harm. For as Paul advises, leave vengeance to God. Holy anger separates one from the cycle of vengeance and violence, and opens up possibility for a creative response that leads to a renewed, more honest relationship between fellow humans and their God. Holy anger thus is never an end in itself. Rather, it is a means to restore relationship and community, and to make love possible once again. If these ends are ever endangered by the character or intention of one's anger, the anger ceases to be holy and becomes vicious.

In order to accomplish its ends, holy anger refuses to break off relationship, even while it may redefine its boundaries. In doing so, holy anger separates me from casting simplistic labels upon those participating in the unjust situation—labels such as "victim," "guilty," "blessed," or "cursed." It makes me aware that both the wrongdoer and I are always in the situation together, and prevents me from demonizing or divinizing either party. This is not a matter of sharing the blame, so much as sharing in the reconciliation. Earlier this year, I had the pleasure of hearing Rev. Dr. Allan Boesak, iconic figure in the struggle against Apartheid in South Africa. He spoke of the radical reconciliation that was made possible by *re-imagining what peace meant* to the people of South Africa. The peace that came out of the Truth and Reconciliation commission was, what Boesak called, a *survivor's* peace. The peace did not depend on avenging the dead, nor in dividing the survivors into victims and oppressors, but brought both black and white South Africans to work as common survivors of Apartheid, to begin the work of reimagining peace together. It was a peace that surpassed understanding, because it surpassed the logic of retribution. It opened a space within which the gospel could speak.

Holy anger redeems the energy of its emotion. Anger is one of the primary emotions we experience as human beings. At the same time, we are right to be wary of its power and the actions that result form it. But to deny it is just as problematic. Why should the sun not go down on your anger, as the saying goes? Because anger itself calls for action, as Aristotle himself noted. To go to sleep angry is to risk preventing the anger from being creatively reinvested into the relationship. Holy anger desires a way to use the energy of anger to reinvest the ground of the relationship with its own truth. When anger is not vicious but holy—as it was between Job and God, Jacob and the angle, and Christ and the people of Jerusalem—it has creative power. Bassett puts it creatively: "This is the best place you can put your anger: your anger is precious to me, it is a thriving plant that I want to prune so that it will bloom and bear fruits of justice and fairness; it is a raw material from which I can and want to make a work of art; it is the most alive part of you which I want to embrace with my life force."[18]

The third and final condition for the virtue of justice to re-imagine anger is that it actively works for reconciliation. The work of reconciliation requires speaking the words of forgiveness. Consider the poem "Feast of Saint Stephen" by Karen Allred McKeever on an everyday experience of anger that takes root in the soul.

> This morning, a sharp wind
> flings tiny ice pellets, hurries
> the dog and me along sidewalks.
> A fitting day to reflect on the first
> Christian martyr. How unlike
> Saint Stephen I am—
> unable to let go a week old
> slight by a fellow parishioner.
> I hold it like a pebble on
> my tongue, taste again
> and again the bitterness
> that would dissolve if only
> I could speak forgiveness.

In a more dramatic example from his book *The End of Memory*, Croatian theologian Miroslav Volf remembers his interrogations by the Communist regime in Yugoslavia in the mid-1980s. He recounts the violence he endured in these interrogations, and strives to understand theologically what it means to remember injustice rightly. Far from minimizing the injustice he suffered at his interrogator's hand, Volf nevertheless asks what effect

18. Bassett, *Holy Anger*.

remembering Christ's Passion has on how we as wronged people remember wrongdoers and our relationship to them?[19] Volf claims that the Passion of Christ requires us to recognize that the grace of God is poured out upon the wronged and the wrongdoer alike. "Christ died for the ungodly," Paul preaches in Romans 5:6. By remembering the Passion of Christ in the midst of justified emotional anger over injustice, we can begin to imagine—only through Christ—how wrongdoers might be remembered as forgiven and as freed from their own vices. Volf, like Christ, seeks redemption, reconciliation, and restoration of right relationship. He is not naïve enough to think that this can always succeed in our lifetime, but to work toward shalom is our calling. Such work is the virtuous activity of justice.

Volf also claims that remembering the Passion of Christ calls us to honor victims while extending grace to the perpetrators of injustice. Only Christ models perfectly what we can struggle to emulate—*both* the truthful condemnation of the offense that protects the suffering, and the gracious return of the offenders to themselves "as children of God."

Lastly, Volf claims, the memory of the Passion offers a way by which reconciliation can occur, even if only partially this side of the eschaton, through genuine repentance on the part of the wrong-doer and forgiveness on the part of the wronged. Volf offers this hope: "The memory of the Passion anticipates the resurrection from death to new life for both the wronged and wrongdoers. . . . The Passion memory anticipates as well the *formation of a reconciled community even out of deadly enemies*."[20]

CONCLUSION

In conclusion, we can say that justice is the virtue of communities and individuals who, through the grace of Christ and rightful truth-telling, participate in the reconciling work of the cross amidst our corporate and personal injustices. In this respect, justice counters the vengeances of vicious anger.

Since virtues and vices swing on common hinges of our humanity, understanding both together opens up ways to being holistically restored as people. Merely blocking, denying, or condemning our vices fails to restore spiritual health within us or love between us. Such simplistic condemnations muddy our insight into our neighbors' humanity and our own, and thus they shatter the fragile ways we uphold the image of God within us. Looking at these virtues and vices together opens up new possibilities to

---

19. Volf, *End of Memory*, 16.
20. Ibid., 119.

reimagine loving our God and our neighbor by appreciating the fragility of our goodness in the face of our desire to live out the Gospel.

That fragility of goodness *within* us necessitates the constant intercession of grace. The fragility of goodness *between* us necessitates the constant extension of grace to each other. This, of course, becomes crucial in the face of deliberate wrongs perpetrated and suffered. Anger and justice are vicious and virtuous ways to respond to sins enacted against one another as persons. As a vice, anger resists the redemptive and restorative work of Christ by becoming consumed with vengeance against the wrongdoer. Justice participates in the redemptive and restorative work of Christ among the people of God by being truthful about the wrongs suffered and working to restore right relationship.

But the world is fallen, and anger does consume individuals and communities. Whatever its path, when vice builds upon vice, and the resistance to a forgiving and loving God is truly entrenched in the soul, the preached words of reconciliation and redemption fall on a hard soil. There may indeed be hardened souls, souls that even the corporate work of justice and reconciliation can barely penetrate, if at all, in this life. In such difficult cases, however, we would do well to remember that justice is only a virtue and not God. Thus, I will end this book with the virtue that is also the name of God—love.

8

ON BEING LOVED

When one asks whether a human being is good, one does not ask what this person believes or hopes, but what he or she loves. The person who loves in the right way, undoubtedly, believes and hopes in the right way. The person who does not love, believes in vain, even though the believed objects are true. The person who does not love, hopes in vain, even though the objects of his or her hope are a real part of true happiness.[1]

—AUGUSTINE

Among the seven holy virtues, love reigns supreme. Throughout the Christian theological tradition, love is consistently named as the pinnacle of the virtues, for it alone endures even after death. It is the alpha and omega of human life. Aquinas declares that love is prior to all the affections of the soul. It is fitting then that we conclude our examination of the seven holy virtues and deadly sins with this virtue that surpasses justice, that endures after all hope has been achieved, that remains once faith takes its final rest when we stand in the presence of God. Indeed, love's highest honor is that it is the very name of God.

And yet, here the difficulties begin. How could something as divine as love be a human virtue? Is love too divine for even the virtues themselves? Christ commands us to love God and neighbor, but how could one

1. Augustine, *Enchiridion* 31.117, quoted in Fitzgerald, *Augustine Through the Ages*, 511.

116

love encompass the eternal and the temporal, the infinite and the finite, the universal and the particular? In examining the virtue of love, we discover both the promise and the limitation of the virtues as a framework for understanding the Christian life. The promise is that all the virtues find unity in love; the limitation is that love *exceeds* the virtues framework of ordered excellence.

Theologically speaking, love encapsulates the whole of the Christian story, centered on the person of Christ, the only perfect revelation of love encountered. As such, we are here reminded that love is no mere emotion, or even act of the will, but a flourishing of the human desire for God in the most fitting manner to our nature, whereby we love God for God's sake, and everything else through that love of God. Consider love's promise as a virtue. Broadly speaking, a moral virtue is a settled disposition of a person to act in excellent and praiseworthy ways, cultivated over time through habit. The constellation of virtues a person may embody provides for a stable organization of one's moral desires directed toward distinct goods. Thus, for example, courage is a particular ordering of desire in the face of threat, which enables a person to overcome the paralysis of fear and the rashness of fearlessness to pursue a just cause. Temperance orders the vital desires for nourishment and sexual intimacy so that the embodied soul may enjoy these desires freely and not become enslaved to them. If every virtue is an ordering of some particular desire, love orders and gives purpose to all human desires. It governs all the virtues. The difficulty in getting a handle on love, however, is that love seems hopelessly vague because of its breadth, or inaccessibly divine because of its transcendence.

That said, in the Christian tradition, the virtue of love that is found in the list of seven is of a particular sort: agape, *caritas*, or charity. This is the distinct form of love introduced by Jesus in his twofold command in Matthew 19, Mark 12, John 13, and most succinctly in Luke 10: "You shall love the Lord your God with all your strength, and with all your mind; and your neighbor as yourself." Combining these two forms of love for God and neighbor, and claiming that the whole of the Old Testament law and prophets rest on these was genuinely something new. This love is not a Greek notion of friendship, a Buddhist notion of compassion, nor a European notion of romantic love. It is a universal love that participates in the reconciliation of all things to God. That said, as a virtue, it must be lived out in our tangible relationships with the particular neighbors before us. The goal of this chapter, therefore, is to bring clarity to encompassing character of the virtue of love, so that we may better live toward the divine *object* of love, God, through our most human neighbor.

Love and Desire

Let us first consider love in its most general form, as it may be directed toward persons or non-persons. *Love is, at base, an inclination, a movement, and a desire to couple two realities: the lover and the beloved.* Love is by its nature *ecstatic*: it stretches outside of ourselves—out from the myopic or self-enclosed world of the "I"—toward that which is loved. As a general affection, love may be directed toward a variety of objects from people to works of art to simple everyday pleasures. We see the beloved object as good, and that goodness provokes passion in us. The passion is not simply one of admiration or respect, but a passion to unite with the beloved.[2] This basic inclination is present in my love of Beethoven sonatas, my wife, and my God. Each is good. Love is thus a desire for some kind of union with the good. Understanding the "coupling" love desires, however, is the key to love being either pathological or healthy, either a moral virtue or a vice.

In general, love's desire is neither a strictly passive nor active movement. We know that at times we cannot choose what or whom we love. Whether we mean something as unformed as a crush felt toward another person or as mature as the love present in a long-lasting marriage, we know that our loves often claim us. With regard for our love of non-personal objects like landscapes, our homes, or works of art, they too lay claim to our attractions and affections prior to our choices. To go on a mountain hike, and to come around a corner of the path revealing a vista of distant valleys and mountains, is a wondrous surprise. In that moment, we don't choose to love, we receive a gift. In an interpersonal context, there are times in long-lasting friendships where one is taken aback at the depth of love for the beloved that wells up spontaneously and anew. Such affections are not chosen; they befall us. Indeed, it would be a sad fate if the birth of all our loves required our will to begin. What a tragic burden for the ego; what a lonely obligation for the individual.

And yet, a love that remains passive, lacking in our own participation, dies in a kind of rapturous paralysis before the beloved. We never take the risk to talk to the person we have the crush on; we never deepen our long standing relationship to a partner. We never achieve union with the good, because we

---

2. "Love pertains to a tendency. . . . When the affection or tendency is wholly inspired by the form of the good that is its object, it takes pleasure in it and adheres to it as though fixed on it, and it is thus said to love it. Whence love is nothing but a certain change of affection toward the beloved. And because everything that is achieved by the form of anything becomes one with it, so through love the one loving is made one with the beloved because this becomes the form of the one loving; (e.g. a friend is another self, becoming one flesh)." Aquinas, *Commentary on Sentences III*, d.27, q.2, a.1–4, quoted in Clark, *Aquinas Reader*, 217.

don't participate in the twofold movement. To some degree, an analogous desire happens with non-personal objects. The purpose of education, say in art
and culture, is to deliberately move beyond our surface and ephemeral likes
and dislikes of pretty things, and to better understand and more deeply feel
the complexity of aesthetic artifacts and performances. Love invites choice,
even if it often doesn't begin with it. Without us consciously taking up the
reality and difficulty of a real relationship, the initial love that promised new
worlds of joy remains stalled at the threshold. All loves are thus inclinations,
movements, or desires to experience the heart of things. They orient our being
to couple with that which is beyond our touch and grasp.

Throughout one's relationship to a loved object or person, love moves
back and forth between passivity and activity, between receptivity and striving. Consider a few lines from Madeline L'Engle's poem "To a Long-Loved
Love."

> We, who have seen the new moon grow old together,
> Who have seen winter rime the fields and stones
> As though it would claim earth and water forever,
> We who have known the touch of flesh and the shape of bones
> Know the old moon stretching its shadows across a whitened
> field
> More beautiful than spring with all its spate of blooms. . . .
> . . . .
> And therefore I find it inexpressibly queer
> That with my own soul I am out of tune,
> And that I have not stumbled on the art
> Of forecasting the weather of the heart.
>
> You are still new, my love. I do not know you.
> Stranger beside me in the dark of bed,
> Dreaming the dreams I cannot ever enter,
> Eyes closed in that unknown, familiar head.[3]

In her address to the beloved with whom she has long dwelled in familiar
and shared hospitality, she knows that her lover also remains hidden and
perpetually and potentially new to her. She is not in control of the revela-
tions her lover offers. Her beloved remains beyond her knowing gaze. If love
is experienced between activity and passivity, it is also experienced between
distance and intimacy. Love exists in *the between*.

Our loves, like anything we are passionate about, provoke us to speak.
A love that is not declared, even in secret to oneself, lacks something

3. L'Engle, "To a Long-Loved One," in *Ordering of Love*, 3–4.

essential. But *how* do we declare a love that fits with the experience of love itself? Is saying "I love you" the best way to speak our love? Contemporary philosopher and linguist Luce Irigaray considers this question. In her book entitled "I Love to You," and the chapter of the same name, Irigaray re-imagines the grammar of our declarations: "I love *to* you" instead of "I love you." By making love an intransitive, rather than a transitive verb, the lover does not enact something upon a passive beloved. The declaration of love becomes less about the *one declaring* and more about the *two coupling*. "I love to you" is akin to "I speak to you" or "I dance with you," wherein both parties participate in love's choreography. In contrast, "I love you, I desire you, I take you, I seduce you, I order you, I instruct you, and so on, always risk annihilating the alterity of the other, of transforming him/her into my property, my object, of reducing him/her to what is mine, into mine."[4]

When we are truly attentive to the experience of love, we know that to love something is to be called into a dialogue, a dialogue as dependent upon listening as speaking. Irigaray attests, "I am listening to you not on the basis of what I know, I feel, I already am, nor in terms of what the world and language already are . . . I am listening to you rather as the revelation of a truth that has yet to manifest itself—yours and that of the world revealed through and by you."[5] To love is to be attentive and to await, it involves a deliberate openness.

These characteristics of the general desires of love disclose an essential fact of finite human life: *we are not that which we love*. We are not creation, we are not other people, and we are not God. Yet we are called to love each, for each is good. At the same time, we are not self-sufficient, nor are we ever truly ourselves as lonely individuals. Loving fits our nature, because we are by nature incomplete beings. The separation between me and others, or me and God, is anxious. Anxiety is part of the human condition and often at play in the ecstatic attraction to couple with another reality or person. To be human is to be distanced or asynchronous from that which is not us. Indeed, to the extent that our inclinations are often divided against our own selves, we are alienated from our own souls. This anxiety can, of course, turn pathological when one attempts to erase the difference between oneself and another, or when vices like lust or envy warp our longing to be with and be like those we love. In this regard, sin is at root the pathological alienation from that which we should love. But anxiety need not be tragic and difference need not be violent. Indeed, virtuous love knows this. Virtuous love redeems our separateness, our individuality, and our distance from others and God.

4. Irigaray, *I Love to You*, 110.
5. Ibid.

LOVE AND THE MORAL LIFE

In order to see the redemptive quality of love, we need language that fits our nature as spiritual beings. So far in our analysis, love has been described in theological terms for the nature of God and psychological terms for a human affection. There is a significant conceptual gulf between these two. Love as a *virtue* offers a way to bridge this dualism of spirit and body. As a virtue, love is an excellence of the human person and community, grounded in the *imago Dei*, whereby we live *as human beings toward God*.

Think back to the scene from *Les Miserable* with which we opened this book, where the priest is confronted at his door by an ex-con seeking hospitality. Why does the bishop exhibit the virtue of love? On the one hand, he displays love toward Jean Valjean because he has been habituated to a life devoted to God by serving the least of God's children. A loving response to the ex-con comes naturally to the bishop; loving others well is part of the bishop's character. But what makes that an act of love as opposed to duty? After the encounter, the bishop does not cultivate an ongoing relationship with Jean Valjean. Could we just as easily explain this as the bishop's honoring his *obligation* to forgive?

To answer this question, consider the trajectory by which we move from immaturity to maturity as Christian disciples. How do we, who are not born virtuous, become so? We become virtuous by moving from being polite, to performing our moral duty, to loving. Let us start at the bottom: to act politely is to act as if one were moral. For example, I struggle to teach my seven-year-old son to demonstrate good manners at the table, which is a way of telling him to "act as if" he really did respect others at the table. Through politeness, otherwise immoral people display a semblance of morality.

Morally upright and dutiful people, however, know they are called to be more than merely polite, for they know what they *ought* to do. They do their duty, obey the prescriptions of the law, and make the right decisions out of that obligation. For example, dutiful people give alms to the poor because it is the right thing to do, not because it earns them respect in the eyes of their peers. Dutiful people do not cheat others out of their rightful due, because such actions would violate some prescribed moral law. There is, however, something higher than duty. André Comte-Sponville insightfully points out that "moral duty does not prescribe love; instead, it asks us to perform out of duty the very same action that, if we loved, we would have accomplished for love alone. Hence duty's maxim: Act as though you loved."[6]

6. Comte-Sponville, *Small Treatise on the Great Virtues*, 224.

Christ reminds us of this higher calling: "By this everyone will know that you are my disciples, if you have love for one another" (John 13:35). Why does Christ not say that others will know us by our obedience to the law? Because, in the end, we as children of God are called to love our neighbors as children of God. If the bishop in *Les Miserables* genuinely acts out of love, then he does not see Jean Valjean as a situation within which he can obey the commandment to love his neighbor; *he sees Valjean, the neighbor, whom he loves through God.*

His virtuous desire is to love God and neighbor, and through that love fulfill the commandment. Politeness, duty and the law have a place in the moral life, yet love is its telos. Thus, while Christ's love is not the law itself, neither does Christ abolish the law. Christ fulfills the law, through love.

FRIENDSHIP AND PARTICULAR LOVES

If love is a desire to couple two realities or two persons, friendship appears the most excellent of human loves. Aristotle's articulation of virtuous friendship continues to influence how we think of this love today. Contemporary sociologist Ray Pahl, in his study of friendship across history and contemporary society, says, "It may thus be claimed that this pure Aristotelian form of friendship constitutes the most complete moral experience of which a human being is capable."[7] According to Aristotle, friendship is itself a virtue as well as a school *for* becoming virtuous. Good friends make each other good. Of course, the opposite would seem true as well: vicious friends encourage each other's vices. But Aristotle would differ, claiming that the vicious do not really have friendships at all, only semblances of them. They are as misguided in their conception of friendship as they are in other areas of life. Genuine friendship is, at root, a relationship between two or more persons in which there is mutually recognized and reciprocated goodwill. Friendships, unlike other loves, essentially tend toward equality, similarity, and proximity. Such love celebrates the goodness of pleasure between friends, and the pleasure of goodness itself. This love is joyful and wishes the best for the friend.

Friendship love begins, as C. S. Lewis succinctly says, in the experience of "What, you, too?!"[8] It begins with the realization that something you care about—a hobby, a sport, a particular artist, a nostalgia—is also the care of another. In this sense, there are as many kinds of friendships as there are possible shared interests between people. Friendships, thus, are a mediation

7. Pahl, *On Friendship*, 22.
8. Lewis, *Four Loves*, 78.

of three: the two friends, and the third thing that unites them. They are not, by nature, jealous if a third person should join in the interest. Whereas romantic love, you might say is, two people gazing into each other's eyes, friendship love is two (or more) people standing side-by-side, gazing into some shared love for something else. It is the direction romantic love must move if it is to last beyond its infancy.

If friendship involves sharing in a common love or concern, the question is, "What is most worth caring about?" According to Aristotle, *virtuous* friends wish the same thing for each other—namely that both will live a good life, in accordance with the same virtues, in accordance with the same understanding of happiness. For Aristotle, it makes no sense to think that two people could achieve complete friendship if they held different views on the nature of happiness, what it means to be human, or what ethics and values are important to embody. In contrast to more modern understandings, Aristotle claims that the highest form of friendship love is not due to shared history, loyalty, suffering, or enjoyment. We love our virtuous friends because they are worthy of our love. And they are worthy of our love because they too love the same good that we love, and try to live according to that good, which makes them good in themselves.

For Aristotle, "The friend is another my-self." On a basic level, my friendship to others is the same as my friendship to myself. Indeed, without the love-of-self, love-of-other-self would be impossible. To say this, however, is not the same thing as the contemporary individualistic conception that I establish my self first, alone, and then go out into the world to find friends who also have already arrived at loving themselves, alone. Rather, it is to say that what I should love in my friend—their embodiment of a virtuous life of goodness—is exactly what I should find and love in me. This is why friendship is the school of virtue.

Of course shared history, memories, and co-habitation enrich and enable friendships. I cannot love some generic or abstract friend, but rather this individual person here. Aristotle is not blind to this reality, but he can teach us something new—namely, that even though I love a friend because of who they are, *who they are* is defined not by their individuality alone but also because they *live a good human life in relationship to me and others*. I admire *their* courage, justice, compassion, hope, wisdom, or love of beauty. Sharing a common commitment to an understanding of the good life unites friends more deeply than anything else. Friendship possess a kind of double vision, like the virtue of prudence, for the universal and the particular.

We began this chapter by saying that among the seven virtues, love reigns supreme. *Philia* is a worthy candidate for such high praise because of the particular way that it couples the two realities of my friend and myself.

To know and commit oneself to a particular friend, to encourage the best in them and they in you, and to establish community through friendships are all some of the greatest goods of this life.

IS THERE A DISTINCT CHRISTIAN LOVE?

Much of what has been said so far in this chapter has no necessary relationship to the Christian faith, even if there are parallels between Aristotlean friendship and Christian friendship. The philosophical question of whether there is a distinct form of Christian love, one separate from friendship or romantic love, is of ongoing concern in the Christian tradition. In the last two centuries, many Christian thinkers—Kierkegaard, Nygren, Lewis, and others—have magnified the difference between Christian love (*agape*) and other forms of love, notably *eros* and *philia*. The reasons for this are not without biblical merit. We read Christ's words in Luke 6:32,

> If you love those who love you, what credit is that to you? For even sinners love those who love them. If you do good to those who do good to you, what credit is that to you? For even sinners do the same. If you lend to those from whom you hope to receive, what credit is that to you? Even sinners lend to sinners, to receive as much again. But love your enemies, do good, and lend, expecting nothing in return.

Certainly Christianity does not dismiss friendship, but because of passages like this and Christ's own life on earth, the Christian tradition recognizes charity as the highest virtue and the *telos* of all other loves.

To highlight the differences between these loves, we look to Kierkegaard's classic *Works of Love*. Kierkegaard, as we have seen before in this book, is one of those incisive Christian thinkers who cuts through any false assumptions about how easy the Christian life might be. Just when we feel good about ourselves, just when we raise up the lofty beauty of the Christian life, its joys, pleasures, and ideals, Kierkegaard speaks the harsh truth of the gospels. Like Martin Luther before him, Kierkegaard reminds us of how radically different the demands of the Christian life are from the life hailed by our society.

In *Works of Love*, Kierkegaard critiques the importance his society attaches to friendship and romantic love, while it dismisses a distinctly Christian form of love. Kierkegaard is particularly critical of the culture of German romanticism and its embrace of the ideal of romantic love, held up in the West since at least the legend of Tristan and Isolde. It is a radically *particular* form of love, involving one individual falling in love with one other individual. This romantic imagination continues today in both secular and Christian contexts. In such an imagination, the beloved is that one unique soulmate, out there in the world, that the lone lover is destined to seek. As the story goes, true love can be realized only in finding that particular love. A Christian version of this is the idea that God has chosen one, and only one, person for each to marry. Kierkegaard comments on these mistaken views of love. "And when a person will go out into the world, he can go a long way—and go in vain—he can wander around the whole world—and in vain—all in order to find the beloved or friend." A similar, albeit weaker, claim can be said of the friend as a kind of non-romantic Aristotlian "soulmate." This is not the mere acquaintance or colleague, but a true and virtuous friend. "It is good fortune, almost as great, to find the one and only friend," writes Kierkegaard.[9] Some of us are blessed to find in this life soulmates or a close network of friendships that are enjoyable and virtuous. But there is no guaruntee that we will.

"But Christianity never suffers a person to go in vain, for when you open the door which you shut in order to pray to God, the first person you meet as you go out is your neighbor whom you *shall* love. You can never confuse him with anyone else, for indeed all people are your neighbor."[10] Christian love, for Kierkegaard, cannot be founded upon fortune or particularity. The freedom that Christian love has is grounded in the fact that it is universal. Just as God is always there for me to love, so is the neighbor. *Agape* loves the neighbor as the concrete other before me here and now. It is both universal and individual: this person here and now shall be loved.

Kierkegaard's second critique of his society's emphasis on friendship and romantic love is that they are preferential. Your friends are those you choose and prefer to be with. They are our families of choice, our personal relationships based upon the qualities, enjoyments, lifestyles, etc. that we prefer in ourselves. Our romantic loves are even more in line with our specific preferences and particular enjoyments. Christian love, however, is based on a commandment—an ethical obligation—you shall love your neighbor! It would be ridiculous to apply this standard to friendship or romantic love. According to his society's view of romantic love, you don't have an obligation to fall in love with your beloved—it would cease to be the passion of romantic love then. Christians are called to renounce themselves, that is, their preferences and choices, so that they may fulfill the commandment to love their neighbor. The virtue of the Christian is not that she loves

9. Kierkegaard, *Works of Love*, 64.
10. Ibid.

her friends, or her beloved—even the pagans do this—but that she loves her neighbor, her enemy, those who persecute her. Friendship as such instills no distinctly Christian virtues in one, and too often it distracts Christians from those virtues that they are commanded to adopt.

Kierkegaard's final critique claims that self-love is the root of friendship and romantic love. Ideally, according to his society, one's friends and lovers become other versions of oneself. They become one flesh. While Aristotle hopes these friendships encourage each other to be their best selves, he also says that the friend is another "my-self." In contrast, *self-renunciation* is the root of neighborly love. The neighbor is always a "you," always something distinct from you, and always someone you cannot be united with. You and your neighbor never achieve the selfishness of intimacy, but you do gain a more spiritual and selfless love. Kierkegaard concludes,

> One's neighbor is one's equal. One's neighbor is not the beloved, for whom you have passionate preference. Nor is your neighbor, if you are well-educated, the well-educated person with whom you have cultural equality—for with your neighbor you have before God the equality of humanity . . . Nor is your neighbor the one who is inferior to you, that is, insofar as he is inferior he is not your neighbor, for to love one because he is inferior to you can very easily be partiality's condenscecension and to that extent self-love. No, to love one's neighbor means equality.[11]

THE PLACE OF LOVE AMONG THE VIRTUES

Kierkegaard's critique of friendship and romantic love is intentionally stark. If Christians preach that God is love, and Christ says that Christians are known by their love, then that love must be distinct from other forms of love and affection. Indeed for Kierkegaard, love reigns supreme over all other virtues. But what exactly does this mean?

First, love is a more necessary virtue than the others. Ideally, we might say that a truly virtuous life entails the flourishing of all our capacities and the realization of our full potential as human beings. Along these lines, we could say that a holistically good human life realizes each of the seven virtues in their fullness. In such a life, one would become truly wise, temperate, just, courageous, hopeful, faithful, and loving. In such a view, happiness, shalom, or salvation is each a way of expressing ideal flourishing.

11. Ibid., 72.

But there are serious questions that arise from such a view. Human existence is not ideal—we are finite and fallen, suffering and mortal, and embedded in imperfect communities and social systems. An ideally virtuous life is not possible. More often than not, due to the vicissitudes of circumstance, the limitations on our time and opportunities, and peculiar personality traits, individuals have strengths in some virtues more than others. The virtues mature unevenly in the soul. Most of us die untimely deaths, where we might wish we had more opportunities to reach some potential, heal some wound, speak some truth, or restore some relationship. Given our mortality, all virtues will not have the opportunity to be exercised. In addition, we each have callings that steer us toward distinct opportunities. So while the *telos* remains to honor one's full humanity through the cultivation of all excellences, most of the time our individual callings strengthen some virtues in us more than others. Thankfully, we might say, human beings live in community where a variety of spiritual gifts come together. Some work for justice, others restore hope, still others cultivate wisdom.

The place of love in the flourishing human life is different than the host of other virtues. No calling in life, no vocation to serve God and neighbor, is possible without love. The degree to which one loves is the degree to which any virtue serves God and neighbor. Love plays a central role in any Christian vocation. Its significance in the Christian life is universal. When Aquinas considers whether love (*caritas*) is a virtue, he notes that different kinds of human lives have different kinds of happiness. A public career enables the happiness of civic life. An academic career offers another kind of intellectual happiness. "But," Aquinas claims, "there is promised to us a certain happiness in which we shall be equal to the angles . . . [I]t is therefore likewise fitting that humanity should arrive at that divine happiness because he has become a participant in divine life. . . . Therefore, it was natural to believe in a kind of friendship with God by which we might enjoy his company, and this is charity (*caritas*)."[12] As Paul puts it in 1 Corinthians, "If I speak in the tongues of mortals and of angels, but do not have love, I am a noisy gong or a clanging cymbal. And if I have prophetic powers, and understand all mysteries and all knowledge, and if I have all faith, so as to remove mountains, but do not have love, I am nothing. If I give away all my possessions, and if I hand over my body so that I may boast, but do not have love, I gain nothing" (13:1–3).

The second aspect of love's relation to other virtues claims that each of the virtues can be understood as distinct ways that a person loves God. *Every virtue is a form of love.* This, you might say, is the simplicity of the

12. Aquinas, *Commentary on Sentences III*, in Clark, *Aquinas Reader*, 217.

virtues. This follows from Christ's statement in the Gospel of Matthew 22:38–39, where all the commandments boil down to two loves, which are really one: love your God with all your heart and your neighbor as yourself. In this sense, all virtues are distinct ways that love is enacted. Augustine writes in *On the Morals of the Catholic Church*,

> As to virtue leading us to a happy life, I hold virtue to be noth-ing else than perfect love of God. For the fourfold division of virtue I regard as taken from four forms of love . . . temperance is love giving itself entirely to that which is loved; fortitude is love readily bearing all things for the sake of the loved object; justice is love serving only the loved object, and therefore ruling rightly; prudence is love distinguishing with sagacity between what hinders it and what helps it. The object of this love is not anything, but only God, the chief good, the highest wisdom, the perfect harmony. So we may express the definition thus: that temperance is love keeping itself entire and incorrupt for God; fortitude is love bearing everything readily for the sake of God; justice is love serving God only, and therefore ruling well all else, as subject to man; prudence is love making a right distinction between what helps it towards God and what might hinder it.[13]

The reason that all virtues aim toward God is that God is love. Thus, as a virtue, love is that excellence of the human person and community, grounded in the *imago Dei*, whereby we live *as human beings toward God* by loving our neighbor.

From 1 John 4:7–12.

> Beloved, let us love one another, because love is from God; everyone who loves is born of God and knows God. Whoever does not love does not know God, for God is love. God's love was revealed among us in this way: God sent his only Son into the world so that we might live through him. In this is love, not that we loved God but that he loved us and sent his Son to be the atoning sacrifice for our sins. Beloved, since God loved us so much, we also ought to love one another. No one has ever seen God; if we love one another, God lives in us, and his love is perfected in us.

---

13. Augustine, *Of the Morals of the Catholic Church*, 15.

Loving Particular Persons

Virtue language sounds beautiful, indeed it should: courage, justice, wisdom, temperance, hope, faith, and love. But it must be lived out in the particular, which is messy, aching, and suffering. While indeed *agape* is a universal love for neighbor, the biblical accounts of it are often in relation to a particular group of people. The Old Testament prophets emphasize loving the MVPs of society—"Most Vulnerable Persons"—namely, the orphans, widows, or strangers. Such peoples were vulnerable not simply because they often lacked economic capital, but more significantly because they lacked social capital. There were most likely to be friendless and without social networks of support. These were the "least of these" that the nation of Israel was called to love. In the New Testament, Christ's more poignant challenge was to love beyond even the most vulnerable, to the point of loving one's enemies and those who would persecute you.

The ancient Greeks thought that even if someone had every intention of being courageous in battle, but never had the opportunity to actually be courageous, he was not courageous. Virtue is a disposition to act and is completed by action. Charity works the same way. Thankfully, the opportunity to love is not as rare as the opportunity to fight, for as Kierkegaard notes "every person you encounter is your neighbor." The Christian need not search the world for the ideal neighbor, the way a romantic might search the world for their ideal bride. No, the neighbor is this person before me here and now. She is there "when I walk out my door." In Kierkegaard's account, as in Christ's own ministry on earth, the universal love of charity is lived out in particular relationships between specific people.

Dostoyevky's *Brothers Karamazov* helps us appreciate this insight. What does charity mean when we are relating to particular people? In Dostoyevsky's novel, Ivan Karamazov, the intellectual skeptic of the three brothers, puts the question most harshly to his younger brother Alyosha, himself training for the ministry. Ivan says that most of us cannot love our neighbors—especially the sick or poor—because of their embodiment and peculiarities. In the words of Ivan, they often look ugly, smell bad, invade our personal space, or have some annoying habit.

> I never could understand how it is possible to love one's neighbors. In my opinion, its precisely one's neighbors that one cannot love. Perhaps if they weren't so nigh. . . . In my opinion, Christ's love for people is in its kind a miracle impossible on earth. . . . Beggars, especially noble beggars, should never show themselves in the street; they should ask for alms through the newspapers. Its still possible to love one's neighbor abstractly,

and even occasionally from a distance, but hardly ever up close. If it were all as it is on stage, in a ballet, where beggars come in silken rags and tattered lace and ask for alms dancing gracefully, well, then it would still be possible to admire them. To admire, but not to love.[14]

In the scene, Alyosha is unsure how to respond to his brother, but earlier in the novel, Alyosha's spiritual mentor, Father Zosima, addresses the same question. Zosima reflects on a doctor he once knew who challenged him with the statement, "I love mankind, but I am amazed at myself: the more I love mankind in general, the less I love people in particular, that is individually, as separate persons. . . As soon as someone is there, close to me, his personality oppresses my self-esteem and restricts my freedom."[15] This is precisely what face-to-face encounters do. They unsettle our freedom and humble our sense of control over the world. Face to face encounters call us to responsibility.

The reason is that particular people demand something of us that abstract people do not. To love one's neighbor is to love this person here, with their unique biography and body. To love the neighbor is to accept the restriction on my own freedom that this person here and now demands. It is not to take the haughty attitude of being "charitable" to the "least of these" from one's own height and power, but to recognize that the other's dignity reigns above our own. It is to say that "I can be Christ to others because in this moment, they are Christ to me." As we said above about the nature of love in general, charity is a relationship involving active and passive movements. To envision charity as simply *me doing something for the neighbor* robs the neighbor and myself of relationship, humanity, and the possibility of reconciliation in the face of difference.

Elsewhere in *The Brothers Karamazov*, Father Zosima counsels another person with a different difficulty. "I sometimes dream of giving up all, all I have, and going to become a sister of mercy. I dream [that I have] an invisible strength in myself. No wounds, no festering sores could frighten me . . . I am ready to kiss those sores." But alas her dream of being committed to a life of love falters. "If the sick man whose sores you are cleansing does not respond immediately with gratitude but, on the contrary, begins tormenting you with his whims, not appreciating and noticing your philanthropic ministry, if he begins to shout at you . . . what then? Will you go on loving, or not?"[16]

14. Dostoyevsky, *Brothers Karamazov*, 237
15. Ibid., 57.
16. Ibid.

Charity's command that we love our enemies often evokes images of loving foreign terrorists, oppressive bosses, or those in our own community who have shamed us. Indeed, charity does call upon us to love such people, as we spoke of in the previous chapter. But Dostoyevsky's character is not wrestling with loving her outright enemies, i.e., those who seek to do her harm, but with loving those who do not show gratitude for her obvious kindness and care. This indeed is probably a more common experience of "loving those who persecute you"—loving those who refuse to acknowledge or show gratitude for the love we are trying to show them. This demand for reciprocity, or more likely, acknowledging the power differential between care-giver and receiver, is foreign to true charity. Charity is love without pity, love without neediness, love without the hierarchy of status. Charity is the virtue that recognizes the equality of the *imago Dei* in the other, respects their dignity before us, and places our own selves in service to their needs. It is a love commanded by the very face of the other. That is to say, such love sees the face of Christ in the particular face of the individual before us..

Charity is not opposed to friendship or romantic love. That said, charity does not demand the satisfaction of like preferences and passions, nor does it require an intimacy that erases all differences. Friendship without charity demands virtuous perfection; romantic love without charity requires continuous passionate union. By cultivating charity in us, we find the neighbor in our friends and lovers. Charity opens a space to love between us and those we are closest to. In our own experiences of those we know, we look at the faces of our parents, our children, our lovers and friends. We desire desperately to find them behind their glances, expressions, and words. We sand away the layers that have been projected, layers we each believe mask something essential. But we also, over time, share a history of scars and stories that layer upon. To live in companionship with another is to write upon each other's visages. These writings give identity to the transcendence that we are called to love. The infinity revealed in others' faces propels both movements—of subtraction and addition, of humility and presumption, of anticipation and memory.

In the end, the virtue of love possesses the courage to meet the neighbor face-to-face knowing that this face reflects the face of Christ. That which is most divine is seen in that which is most human. In such moments, the incarnation is disclosed again in the *imago Dei* before me. And we, like Peter on the beach following Christ's resurrection, are given the opportunity to reconcile with our God once more. The neighbor's vulnerability, their own emptying of self, calls us to love. The Jewish philosopher Emmanuel Levinas states it thus:

The epiphany of the Absolute Other is a face by which the Other challenges and commands me through his nakedness, through his destitution. He challenges me from his humility and his height. He sees but remains invisible. . . . Nothing which concerns this Stranger can leave the I indifferent. It forbids me from exercising this responsibility [for him] as pity, for I must render an account to the very one for whom I am accountable.[17]

When we look back to the seven deadly vices, we see another aspect of love's supremacy. In the course of the previous chapters, we have paired individual vices with virtues to reveal their characteristics in new and significant ways. Love, however, cannot be paired so easily with any single vice. Many would contrast love with lust, but such a comparison reduces love simply to a solution to our disordered sexual desire. In this view, love would not merit the suffering and death of God on a cross. Others might contrast love with anger or vengeance. Such a love, however, reduces love to a pacifying role amidst our emotional tumult. Such a love could not become the creative force that the Christian community has exhibited throughout history.

No, love stands alone as the greatest of the virtues because it speaks restoration into the ears of all the vices. Love grounds the proud, invigorates the slothful, abates the gluttonous, edifies the lustful, emancipates the greedy, centers the envious, and redeems the angry. Love hides a multitude of sins (1 Peter 4:8).

Love not only commands the seven vices; it reorients how we think about the seven virtues as well. The language of the virtues, in their emphasis on the perfection of human excellences, always runs the risk of over-glorifying human capacities. Aristotle's description of friendship, noble as it is, fits with this perfectionist tendency in virtue ethics. Virtuous friendship, in this view, perfects the self. But the Christian faith requires a dying of self. Set within the Christian story of redemption through Christ, love humbles the refined excellences of the virtues and reminds us of our dependence on God. In love we not only move from vice to virtue, but from virtue to grace.

Looking back at the six other virtues, we can see that in love, wisdom is not simply intellectual mastery, but humility before truth. Faith is not mere proclamation, but receptivity to God's grace. Temperance is not strictly restraint of pleasures, but the capacity to enjoy our vitality in community with others. Through love, hope entails trembling, courage includes woundedness, and justice seeks restoration. But how does love accomplish this reorientation? Because love is not simply the greatest of the human virtues; it is greater than virtue itself. Love is divine.

17. Levinas, "Transcendence and Height," 17–19.

LOVE AS GIFT

We concluded the previous chapter on anger and justice with the follow-ing: "Whatever its path, when vice builds upon vice, and the resistance to a forgiving and loving God or neighbor is truly entrenched in the soul, the preached words of reconciliation and redemption fall on a hard soil." Some-times in our lives, we undergo offenses and suffering that damage our souls more deeply than some stolen silver and rejected hospitality did for the bishop in *Les Miserables*. At times we experience sins we can barely endure, relationships so broken we can no longer hope, and abuses to our person that seem to condemn our very identity. In these moments, we stagger be-fore the task of cultivating within ourselves a loving and forgiving soul over time through habit. To love another with charity seems impossible. A virtu-ous life seems beyond our capacity, when for poverty of spirit or sustenance, we barely can think past today.

Let us return to the story with which we began our examination in this book, Victor Hugo's novel *Les Misérables*. The story recounts the fall and redemption of a convicted thief, Jean Valjean. Originally a morally good person of little financial means, Valjean is sentenced to five years for steal-ing a loaf of bread to feed his family. Over nineteen years of incarceration, however, Valjean's moral character changes from virtue to vice, from one inclined to seek goodness to one habituated to do evil. Upon being released from prison, he is friendless, without money or food, and carries within himself an acute awareness of his own desperate and contemptible state.

As you recall, Valjean is directed to a bishop in town who is known for his exceptional and long-standing humility, kindness, and good works for the poor and friendless in society. Seemingly without hesitation, Bish-op Myriel receives the convict and bestows dignity upon him by looking Valjean in the eye, sharing a meal at the house table using their finest silver, and inviting him to sleep the night in a bed with clean sheets. Despite be-ing returned to this long forgotten state of goodness, in the middle of the night he steals the bishop's silver and flees. The graces offered by the bishop are stolen away by Valjean. After Valjean is caught by police, there is no reason for the Bishop to speak out against the "justice" due Valjean. The bishop's virtue, however, does not allow that to happen. In keeping with his own character, the bishop forgives the convict. In the act of forgiveness, the virtuous priest gives to the vicious convict Jean Valjean's own virtue, his own good soul that was lost in memory over those nineteen years but now given back. Upon granting forgiveness, Bishop Myriel says to Valjean, "Now, go in peace. . . . Forget not, never forget that you have promised me to use this silver to become a better man. . . . Jean Valjean, my brother, you belong no longer to evil, but to good. It is your soul that I am buying for you. I withdrew it from dark thoughts and from the spirit of perdition and I give it to God."[18]

To be given to God. To be given to love. For the Christian, hope is not lost when we remember that love is beyond human virtue. Love is a gift—a grace from God—that transcends our habits, our history, and our limited capacity to move beyond sin.

Why is love a gift, not merely a virtue? A virtue is an excellence internal to the self or community, cultivated over time through habit. A gift transcends the self, and offers the individual something beyond one's own capacities. When such grace comes, it would not be accurate to say that the ability to forgive and the ability to receive forgiveness, the ability to hope and the ability to offer hope, are the result of obligation or of virtue. Rather, it is only from a divine gift to the offender and offended alike that reconciliation and restoration are attained. Love intervenes, not always as love internal to either, but as a love outside of and higher than both.

Charity originates from plentitude, not lack, and from generosity, not preferential similarity. God's love for us, or my love for my children, or my neighbors' unmerited love for me, are gifts. Christian philosopher James Olthuis writes, in *The Hermeneutics of Charity*,

> Love as gift creates a space-which-is-meeting, inviting partnership and co-birthing. Beginning with love as a creative power (making something out of nothing) gives new place to love as forgiveness (making nothing out of something). In the experience of forgiveness, there is release, a letting go, a freeing to new starts and new creations. Love turns us to the other, not as diminution of being, but as *enrichment, hospitality, and celebration*."[19]

Among the truly virtuous and saintly souls it is difficult for us to see the *giftedness* of love moving through them. The saints possess the excellence of character to incorporate the divine gift into their natural movements with such elegance that none but they know how they tremble in their hearts before the task. They know that beyond the movement from vice to virtue is the movement form virtue to grace. For the rest of us, who face the terrifying commission of breaking free from sin and fallen relationships, it is a blessing that we need not rely on duty or virtue alone, but may find the strength to love from the source of love itself. "We love because he first loved us" (1 John 4:19).

18. Hugo, *Les Miserables*, 106.
19. Olthuis, in Smith and Venema, *Hermeneutics of Charity*, 37–38.

BENEDICTION

Martin Luther King Day, 2014

W HEN I WAS A child at North Park Covenant Church on the North Side of Chicago, there was a time when our pastor would preach to us that *we were called to be saints*. Not simply good people, churchgoers, or even Christians, but *saints*. In fact, he said, that's the only calling there is. That's a tall order for a boy to hear, especially when I wasn't even sure what the word meant.

In November of each year, on All Saints Day, my church did, and still does, hang throughout the sanctuary immense black-and-white posters of these saints. Throughout Christian history, icons have been used to teach the faith without words by giving us a language of images. So for a while there, I still didn't know what the word saint meant, but I had these images, this gallery of icons, this communion of saints, that I sat among every November.

Among these icons weren't simply the old church fathers and mothers, but others like Dietrich Bonhoeffer, Rosa Parks, and Martin Luther King Jr. "Ah these I know from school," I thought; "these were the heroes of democracy, civil rights, and liberty. I get it, saints are heroes."

But there, in church, standing under these pictures of King and Rosa Parks, we filled the sanctuary with song: "For all the Saints who from their labors rest, who thee, by faith, before the world confessed, Thy name oh Jesus, be forever blessed, Alleluia." Something different was going on. I was beginning to see that we sang not only to honor any individual pictured above, though we had our favorites, but also to honor the faithfulness of the communion of saints—all of them, together.

Much later in life, while teaching at North Park University, I read the Anglican minister Sam Wells. Reverend Wells points out that the word for hero never appears in the New Testament. The word for saint appears sixty-four times.

A hero is always the center of the story. Without them, everything would go wrong. The story of a saint, by contrast, is really a story about God, so much so that saints are often missed. The icon of a hero is the soldier, who faces a glorious death in battle. The icon of the saint is a martyr, who faces an inglorious death for the just cause. A hero stands out and apart from their community, and in a moment of crisis can depend only on themselves. The saint knows their own frailty and thus depends on and bears witness to the beloved community. As Sam Wells writes, "Of those 64 references to saint in the New Testament, all of them are in the plural. Saints are never alone."[1]

Perhaps our vocation is to be saints. Karl Olson, a formative thinker in my own denomination's history, whose picture hung in my church on those feast days, wrote in his book on *Seven Sins and Seven Virtues*, "I have been given courage to write on saintliness. It is a vexed subject. The pruning and praying of the life tree of the Christian is not so majestic a theme as its planting. But now and then it is well to remind ourselves that sanctity is good and should be given attention."[2]

As we seek inspiration and courage for our own work for peace, justice, and love, we realize that to be a saint is to be ready to forego even the heroic. It is to realize that if we are to be inspired by saints like King and Parks, Bonhoeffer and Augustine, we do so not so much as individuals imitating individuals, but communities joining with communities in love. In the words from the hymn, "O blest communion, fellowship divine! We feebly struggle, they in glory shine; yet all are one in thee, for all are thine. Alleluia!"

1. Wells, *Improvisation*, 22.
2. Olson, *Seven Sins and Seven Virtues*, 9.

BIBLIOGRAPHY

Althaus, Paul. *The Theology of Martin Luther*. Translated by Robert C. Schultz. Minneapolis: Fortress, 1966.

Anselm. *Proslogion*. In *The Major Works*, edited by B. Davies and G. R. Evans. Oxford: Oxford University Press, 1998.

Aquinas. *Summa Contra Gentiles*. Notre Dame: University of Notre Dame Press, 1975.

Aristotle. *Nicomachean Ethics*. Translated by Martin Ostwald. Upper Saddle River, NJ: Prentice Hall, 1999.

———. *Rhetoric*. In *The Basic Works of Aristotle*, edited by R. McKeon. New York: Random House, 1968.

Arlidge, John. "I'm Doing 'God's Work.' Meet Mr Goldman Sachs." *Sunday Times*, November 8, 2009. http://www.law.harvard.edu/programs/corp_gov/MediaMentions/11-8-09_SundayTimes.pdf.

Augustine. *Confessions*. Translated by Henry Chadwick. New York: Oxford University Press, 2009.

———. *De Trinitate*. Washington, DC: Catholic University of America Press, 1963.

———. *Enchiridion (Faith, Hope and Love)*. New Advent. http://www.newadvent.org/fathers/1302.htm.

———. *Homilies on the First Epistle of John*. Christian Classics Ethereal Library. http://www.ccel.org/ccel/schaff/npnf107.

———. *Of the Morals of the Catholic Church*. New Advent. http://www.newadvent.org/fathers/1401.htm.

Basset, Lytta. *Holy Anger: Jacob, Job, Jesus*. Grand Rapids: Eerdmans, 2007.

Bernard of Clairvaux. *Commentary on the Song of Songs*. Etext arranged by Darrell Wright. Internet Archive. https://archive.org/details/StBernardsCommentaryOnTheSongOfSongs.

Berry, Wendell. *The Art of the Commonplace*. Edited by Norman Wirzba. Berkeley: Counterpoint, 2002.

Blackburn, Simon. *Lust: Seven Deadly Sins*. New York: Oxford University Press, 2004.

Bonzo, Matthew, and Michael Stevens. *Wendell Berry and the Cultivation of Life: A Reader's Guide*. Grand Rapids: Brazos, 2008.

Bourke, Vernon J. *Augustine's Love of Wisdom: An Introspective Philosophy*. West Lafayette, IN: Purdue University Press, 1992.

Cheney, Jim. "Eco-Feminism and Deep Ecology." *Environmental Ethics* 9 (1987) 115–45.

Clark, Mary T., ed. *An Aquinas Reader*. New York: Fordham University Press, 2000.

Comte-Sponville, André. *A Small Treatise on the Great Virtues*. Translated by Catherine Temerson. New York: Henry Holt, 2001.

DeYoung, Rebecca. *Glittering Vices*. Grand Rapids: Brazos, 2009.

Dostoyevsky, Fyodor. *The Brothers Karamazov*.

Dyson, Michael Eric. *Pride*. New York: Oxford University Press, 2006.

Eberstadt, Mary. "Is Food the New Sex?" *Policy Review*, January 27, 2009. http://www.hoover.org/research/food-new-sex.

Elrod, John W. "Passion, Reflection, and Particularity." In *Two Ages*, edited by Robert L. Perkins. International Kierkegaard Commentary 14. Macon, GA: Mercer University Press, 1984.

Epstein, Joseph. *Envy: The Seven Deadly Sins*. New York: Oxford University Press, 2006.

Ferguson, Harvie. *Melancholy and the Critique of Modernity: Søren Kierkegaard's Religious Psychology*. New York: Routledge, 1995.

Fitzgerald, Allan D. *Augustine Through the Ages: An Encyclopedia*. Grand Rapids: Eerdmans, 1999.

Gadamer, Hans-Georg. "The Relevance of the Beautiful." In *The Relevance of the Beautiful and Other Essays*, translated by Nicholas Walker, edited by Robert Bernasconi. Cambridge: Cambridge University Press, 1987.

Guignon, Charles. *On Being Authentic*. London: Routledge, 2004.

Hauerwas, Stanley. *The Hauerwas Reader*. Edited by John Berkman and Michael Cartwright. Durham: Duke University Press, 2001.

Hugo, Victor. *Les Miserables*. Translated by Norman Denny. New York: Penguin, 1987.

Irigaray, Luce. *I Love to You: Sketch for a Felicity within History*. Translated by Alison Martin. New York: Routledge, 1996.

Jaeger, Werner. *Paideia: The Ideals of Greek Culture*. Vol. 1. New York: Oxford University Press, 1967.

Jung, L. Shannon. *Sharing Food: Christian Practices of Enjoyment*. Minneapolis: Fortress, 2006.

Kierkegaard, Søren. *Either/Or*. Translated by Howard V. Hong and Edna H. Hong. Princeton: Princeton University Press, 1989.

————. *Provocations: Spiritual Writings of Søren Kierkegaard*. Edited by Charles E. Moore. Maryknoll, NY: Orbis, 2003.

————. *This Present Age*. Translated by Alexander Dru. New York: Harper & Row, 1962.

————. *Two Ages*. Translated by Howard V. Hong and Edna H. Hong. Princeton: Princeton University Press, 2009.

————. *Works of Love*.

King, Martin Luther Jr. "Honoring Dr. Du Bois." In *Freedomways Reader: Prophets in Their Own Country*, edited by Esther Cooper Jackson, 31–39. Boulder, CO: Westview, 2000.

————. *Stride Toward Freedom: The Montgomery Story*. Boston: Beacon, 2010.

————. *A Testament of Hope: The Essential Writings of Martin Luther King, Jr.* Edited by James M. Washington. New York: Harper & Row, 1986.

Kreider, Tim. "The 'Busy' Trap." *New York Times*, July 20, 2012. http://opinionator.blogs.nytimes.com/2012/06/30/the-busy-trap/?_php=true&_type=blogs&_r=0.

Lane, Robert E. *The Loss of Happiness in Market Democracies*. New Haven: Yale University Press, 2001.

L'Engle, Madeleine. *The Ordering of Love: The New and Collected Poems of Madeleine L'Engle*. Colorado Springs, CO: Shaw, 2005.

Levinas, Emmanuel. "Transcendence and Height." In *Emmanuel Levinas: Basic Philosophical Writings*, edited by Adriaan T. Peperzak et al. Bloomington: Indiana University Press, 1996.

Lewis, C. S. *The Four Loves*. Orlando, FL: Harcourt, 1988.

————. "Scraps." In *God in the Dock: Essays on Theology and Ethics*. Edited by Walter Hooper. Grand Rapids: Eerdmans, 1970.

Luther, Martin. *The Babylonian Captivity*. In *Works of Martin Luther: With Introductions and Notes*, edited by Henry Eyster Jacobs and Adolf Spaeth, 2:. Philadelphia: A. J. Holman, 1915.

————. *The Large Catechism of Martin Luther*. New York: Classic Books, 2010.

————. *Luther's Works*. Vol. 31. Edited by Helmut T. Lehmann. Minneapolis: Fortress, 1957.

————. "The Sermon on the Mount." In vol. 21 of *Luther's Works*. Translated by Jaroslav Pelikan. St. Louis: Concordia, 1956.

Lyman, Stanford M. *The Seven Deadly Sins: Society and Evil*. Rev. ed. Dix Hills, NY: General Hall, 1989.

MacIntyre, Alasdair. *After Virtue*. 3rd ed. Notre Dame: Notre Dame University Press, 2007.

Mattison, William C. *Introducing Moral Theology: True Happiness and the Virtues*. Grand Rapids: Brazos, 2008.

McCloskey, Deirdre. *The Bourgeois Virtues. Ethics for an Age of Commerce*. Chicago. University of Chicago Press, 2007.

Nagel, Thomas. "What Is It Like to Be a Bat?" *Philosophical Review* 83 (1974) 435–51.

Norris, Kathleen. *Acedia and Me*. New York: Penguin, 2008.

Nussbaum, Martha. "Objectification." *Philosophy and Public Affairs* 24 (1995) 249–91.

O'Connor, Flannery. *The Complete Stories*. New York: Farrar, Straus and Giroux. 1971.

Olson, Karl A. *Seven Sins and Seven Virtues*. New York: Harper, 1962.

Olthuis, James. "Crossing the Threshold: Sojourning Together in the Wild Spaces of Love." In *The Hermeneutics of Love*, edited by James K. A. Smith and Henry Isaac Venema. Grand Rapids: Brazos, 2004.

Pahl, Ray. *On Friendship*. Malden, MA: Blackwell, 2000.

Pallasmaa, Juhani. *The Eyes of the Skin*. Chichester, UK: Wiley-Academy, 2005.

Paris, Peter. *Virtues and Values: The African American Experience*. Minneapolis: Augsburg, 2004.

Perkins, Robert L. "Envy as Personal Phenomenon and as Politics." In *Two Ages*, edited by Robert L. Perkins. International Kierkegaard Commentary 14. Macon, GA: Mercer University Press, 1984.

Pieper, Josef. *A Brief Reader on the Virtues of the Human Heart*. San Francisco: Ignatius, 1991.

————. *Faith, Hope, Love*. Translated by Mary Frances McCarthy. New York: Random House, 1991.

————. *The Four Cardinal Virtues: Prudence, Justice, Fortitude, Temperance*. Translated by Richard and Clara Winston et al. New York: Harcourt, Brace & World, 1965.

————. "Work, Spare Time, and Leisure." In *Only the Lover Sings: Art and Contemplation*. Translated by Lothar Krauth. San Francisco: Ignatius, 1990.

Porter, Jean. "Virtue Ethics." In *The Cambridge Companion to Christian Ethics*, edited by Robin Gill, 87–102. Cambridge: Cambridge University Press, 2001.

Rubio, Julie Hanlon. *Family Ethics: Practices for Christians*. Washington, DC: Georgetown University Press, 2010.

Sayers, Dorothy. *Letters to a Diminished Church: Passionate Arguments for the Relevance of Christian Doctrine*. Nashville: W Publishing, 2004.

Schabner, Dean. "Americans Work More than Anyone." *ABCNews.com*, May 1, 2014. http://abcnews.go.com/US/story?id=93364.

Schoeck, Helmut. *Envy: A Theory of Social Behavior*. Translated by Michael Glermy and Betty Ross. New York: Harcourt, Brace & World, 1969.

Smith, Greg. "Why I Am Leaving Goldman Sachs." *New York Times*, March 14, 2012. http://www.nytimes.com/2012/03/14/opinion/why-i-am-leaving-goldman-sachs. html?pagewanted=all.

Smith, James K. A., and Henry Isaac Venema. *The Hermeneutics of Charity: Interpretation, Selfhood, and Postmodern Faith*. Grand Rapids: Brazos, 2004.

Solomon, Robert C., and Kathleen Higgins. *What Nietzsche Really Said*. New York: Schocken, 2000.

Taylor, Astra. *Examined Life: Excursions with Contemporary Philosophers*. New York: New Press, 2009.

Taylor, Gabriele. *Deadly Vices*. New York: Oxford University Press, 2006.

Thurman, Robert. *Anger: The Seven Deadly Sins*. New York: Oxford University Press, 2005.

Tolstoy, Leo. "How Much Land Does a Man Need?" *The Literature Network*. http://www.online-literature.com/tolstoy/2738/.

Thurman, Robert A. *Anger: The Seven Deadly Sins*. New York: Oxford University Press, 2006.

Vallicella, William F. "Divine Simplicity." *Stanford Encyclopedia of Philosophy*. http://plato.stanford.edu/entries/divine-simplicity/.

Volf, Miroslav. *Free of Charge: Giving and Forgiving in a Culture Stripped of Grace*. Grand Rapids: Zondervan, 2005.

Wells, Samuel. *Improvisation: The Drama of Christian Ethics*. Grand Rapids: Brazos, 2004.

West, Cornel. "Catastrophic Love." *Big Think*. http://bigthink.com/videos/cornel-wests-catastrophic-love.

White, Richard. *Radical Virtues: Moral Wisdom and the Ethics of Contemporary Life*. Lanham, MD: Rowman & Littlefield, 2008.

INDEX